W9-AJU-829

THE BATTLE OF
BENNINGTON
SOLDIERS & CIVILIANS

MICHAEL P. GABRIEL
Foreword by Tyler Resch

THE
History
PRESS

Published by The History Press
Charleston, SC 29403
www.historypress.net

Copyright © 2012 by Michael P. Gabriel
All rights reserved

Front cover: *The Battle of Bennington 1777*, by Don Troiani,
www.historicalimagebank.com

Back cover: Image courtesy of the National Archives, #148-GW-137.

First published 2012
Second printing 2014

Manufactured in the United States

ISBN 978.1.60949.515.2

Gabriel, Michael P., 1962-
The Battle of Bennington : soldiers and civilians / Michael P. Gabriel.
p. cm.
ISBN 978-1-60949-515-2
1. Bennington, Battle of, N.Y., 1777. 2. Bennington, Battle of, N.Y., 1777--Sources.
3. United States--History--Revolution, 1775-1783--Sources. I. Title.
E241.B4G33 2012
973.3'33--dc23
2011049241

Notice: The information in this book is true and complete to the best of our knowledge. It is offered without guarantee on the part of the author or The History Press. The author and The History Press disclaim all liability in connection with the use of this book.

All rights reserved. No part of this book may be reproduced or transmitted in any form whatsoever without prior written permission from the publisher except in the case of brief quotations embodied in critical articles and reviews.

Contents

CONTENTS

MAPS

FOREWORD

HISTORICAL POINTILLISM

Michael Gabriel has achieved an entirely new and intriguing approach to the reporting of a historic battle. He has focused in detail on the very people who participated in the bloody event—in this case, the brief but turning point Battle of Bennington, which took place on a warm Saturday afternoon in August 1777 on a series of hillsides a few miles west of the Vermont border near the hamlet of Walloomsac, New York.

By laborious scrutiny of Revolutionary War pension applications—comparing one man's recollections with those of others—plus data from town histories, personal correspondence, newspaper accounts, first-person narratives and interviews with participants by such figures as Dr. Asa Fitch and future Vermont governor Hiland Hall, Gabriel has painted a canvas that might be likened to the concept of artistic pointillism, composed of thousands of tiny bits that allow the viewer to take in lots of detail and then stand back to gain a new perspective and understanding of the overall message. The difference is that in historical pointillism, the small components are as rewarding as the canvas itself. The detailed accounts cover demographics, motivations, friendships and other relationships.

Gabriel's technique provides an innovative and very personal understanding of a particular battle, an event that has evoked over many years a stirring sense of patriotism. After all, the Battle of Bennington clearly demonstrated a vigorous cohesiveness and sense of American independence among the early settlers of southern New Hampshire and Vermont and reaching over into Berkshire and Worcester Counties of Massachusetts. One might extend that thought by considering the aura of sturdy independence exhibited a decade later during the tax-revolt episodes known as Shays' Rebellion.

Having served in the Battle of Bennington was an enormous reputation-enhancer during the early nineteenth century in New England, and many were the legends handed down through generations of families—some true and others fanciful. Proof of the erroneous nature of many family stories can be seen in dozens of the four-by-six cards in the Bennington Museum library's file of battle participants, real or alleged. This file was assembled as a 1936 Works Progress Administration project. Many are the cards that list a soldier's name, hometown, military record and the typed conclusion: "He was not at the Battle of Bennington."

Gabriel wisely chose to reproduce the writing of battle participants without correcting spelling, punctuation or grammatical errors. The result is that reading their poignant individual recollections, one after the other in their own misspelled and often awkward phrases—though sometimes articulate and even erudite—brings to brilliant life the chaos and cruelty of warfare, which is, after all, a license to maim and murder.

This book makes a major contribution not only to a profound understanding of the early cohesion of American independence but also, in a larger sense, to the nature of warfare anywhere and any time.

Tyler Resch
Librarian, Bennington Museum

PREFACE

The past decade has witnessed a tremendous interest in the Greatest Generation, the men and women who fought and won World War II. Numerous books and articles have appeared on this subject, and many towns and organizations have begun oral history projects to record their experiences. A similar phenomenon occurred during the first half of the nineteenth century, when another "greatest generation" began to exit the stage. As increasing numbers of Revolutionary War veterans entered their twilight years, Americans attempted to show their gratitude to them and preserve their stories. Congress passed the first federal pension for Continental army veterans in 1818 and then expanded this to cover those who served in the militia. As part of the application process, veterans or their widows had to provide evidence of military service. This frequently included narratives describing their enlistment records.[1] Meanwhile, others such as Hiland Hall, the future governor of Vermont, and local historian Dr. Asa Fitch interviewed veterans and their families to find out what life was really like during the country's founding. The pension act and the efforts of Hall, Fitch and many others preserved a virtual gold mine of firsthand accounts of the Revolutionary era. Still, many people have never seen or even heard of them.

The following book brings together over fifty pension records, interviews and published accounts of an overlooked event from the War for Independence, the Battle of Bennington. On August 16, 1777, a motley collection of militia led by John Stark and supported by Seth Warner's Green

Above: Southeast view circa 1900 from the hill where the dragoon breastwork stood on the Bennington Battlefield. The Walloomsac River lies in the tree line near the center, while the Bennington Battle Monument is visible on the far right. The Tory Redoubt would have been located immediately to the right of this view, beyond the river. *Author's collection.*

Below: Current view from approximately the same location as the previous picture. The Vermont Monument is located in the center. *Author's collection.*

Alexander Magoon's Pension Deposition. *Author's collection.*

Mountain Boys regiment won a critical engagement that changed the war. Bennington halted British general John Burgoyne's march toward Albany and rejuvenated the American cause on the northern front. By the time Burgoyne resumed his advance nearly a month later, thousands of additional American troops had joined Horatio Gates's army near Stillwater, New York. They turned back Burgoyne's attacks at Freeman's Farm on September 19 and at Bemis Heights on October 7, leading to his ultimate surrender at Saratoga ten days later. Saratoga marked a turning point in the war. It offset the loss of Philadelphia in September 1777 and, more importantly, convinced France that the Americans could win their independence. France signed a military alliance with the fledgling United States in February 1778 that transformed a colonial rebellion within the British Empire into a world war. None of this would have been possible without Bennington. Indeed, Lord George Germain, the British war minister, referred to the battle as "fatal," while Thomas Jefferson wrote that it was "the first link in that chain of successes which issued in the surrender at Saratoga."[2]

This book is designed for both the general public and students and scholars of the Revolutionary era to give them an overview of the Battle of Bennington. The documents, many of which were not previously published, also illustrate different dimensions of the War for Independence more generally. They reveal something about how men were selected to serve, why they did so and their experiences on the battlefield. Additionally, the firsthand accounts offer a glimpse into such issues as health, as soldiers were away from home and exposed to disease, and even literacy. The Revolutionary War affected not only the soldiers but also their families. The documents provide insights and give a voice to the wives, brothers, sisters and children left behind. The documents also include selections written by Burgoyne, the two principal German officers at Bennington and some of the Loyalists who supported them to offer a view from the other side. Ideally, the book should also include Canadian and Native American accounts, but few of these exist.[3] Overall, these firsthand accounts allow readers to learn more about this crucial engagement and the real people who lived it.

I would like to thank the following people and organizations for helping make this book possible. The Kutztown University Research and Sabbatical Committees provided me with grants and time to develop this project, as did the James A. and Ruth D. Neff Historical Foundation. NewsBank-Readex and Microform Academic Publishers granted me permission to reprint documents found in their *Early American Newspapers* and British Records Relating to America in Microfilm, respectively. The Bennington Museum allowed me to publish a number of veteran interviews found in its Hall Park McCullough Collection. Beyond this, Tyler Resch has been a strong supporter of my research and made the Bennington Museum library's many resources available to me. The same can be said for Kathie Ludwig, Richard Ryerson, Meg McSweeney and the entire staff of the David Library of the American Revolution, past and present, where I was fortunate enough to spend a month as a research fellow. Located in Washington Crossing, Pennsylvania, the David Library possesses an amazing collection of both primary and secondary sources and is a must for anyone truly interested in researching the Revolutionary era.

My friends Thomas K. Tate, Bernadette Heiney, Michael D. Gambone and Tricia Kelleher read drafts of the manuscript, and their natural good sense and appreciation of history made it a stronger book. My thanks also go to Philip Lord Jr., whose knowledge of the battlefield is unparalleled. He gave George Quintal Jr., a student of the engagement, and me a personal tour of the site. I also thank Lion Miles for generously sharing the insights that he gained after thirty-plus years of studying the battle. I would be remiss not to acknowledge Whitney Tarella, my editor at The History Press, for making the publishing process clear and simple.

Several people and organizations proved instrumental in allowing me to obtain maps and illustrations for this book. The Saratoga National Military Park granted me permission to publish excerpts of Dr. Asa Fitch's notebook, along with his map of the Bennington Battlefield. My thanks also go to Thomas M. Barker and Paul R. Huey for the use of the Northern Campaign map and to the National Archives, the Library of Congress and the Granger Collection, New York, for images found in their collections. Kutztown University's Anne Manmiller, the Department of History's secretary; Bo Zigner, instructional designer; and student monitors in the Department of Communication Design's print laboratory provided me with invaluable technical assistance by scanning maps and illustrations for publication. Phyllis Chapman, the former site coordinator at the Bennington Battlefield Visitor Center, generously sent me a number of excellent photographs of the battleground and nearby monument when my own turned up missing. My friend and former student Steven Grenz gave me a priceless collection of postcards of the Bennington Battlefield that has strengthened my understanding of the engagement

Finally, my sincere love and gratitude go to my wife, Sandy, and our daughter, Katie. Sandy has heard more about the Battle of Bennington and pension records than she ever imagined possible. Still, she was always ready to hear more and gladly allowed these topics to become part of our lives. Katie was born during the early stages of this project, and at age three weeks, she attended my first presentation on the battle. It has been my great delight to show her different parts of the country as she continues to accompany me on my Bennington research.

Michael P. Gabriel
Blandon House
September 15, 2011

The Bennington Expedition

An Overview

War returned to the Champlain Valley in the summer of 1777 as the American Revolution entered its third year. Two years earlier, General Richard Montgomery led an American army north along this traditional invasion path in a failed attempt to conquer Quebec. In October 1776, Sir Guy Carleton, the British governor of Canada, moved south on Lake Champlain trying to capture Fort Ticonderoga and crush the sputtering American rebellion. After defeating Benedict Arnold's lake fleet at Valcour Island, however, Carleton retreated to Canada due to the lateness of the season. The following summer, Britain tried again. By mid-June, Lieutenant General John Burgoyne had assembled an eight-thousand-man army composed of British and German regulars, Loyalists, Canadians and Native Americans at the northern end of the lake. Burgoyne planned to advance south from Canada to Albany, New York, gathering additional strength from the many Loyalists who reputedly lived in the area. There, he would rendezvous with Colonel Barry St. Leger's force advancing east through the Mohawk Valley and Sir William Howe's army moving north from New York City.[4]

Burgoyne's campaign opened auspiciously when, on July 5, he forced the Americans to evacuate Fort Ticonderoga without a fight. He pursued part of their army to Skenesborough, New York, on South Bay, where the colonists hastily abandoned several hundred bateaux and other vessels loaded with military equipment. Meanwhile, other British and German troops scattered the American rear guard, commanded by Colonel Seth Warner, in a sharp

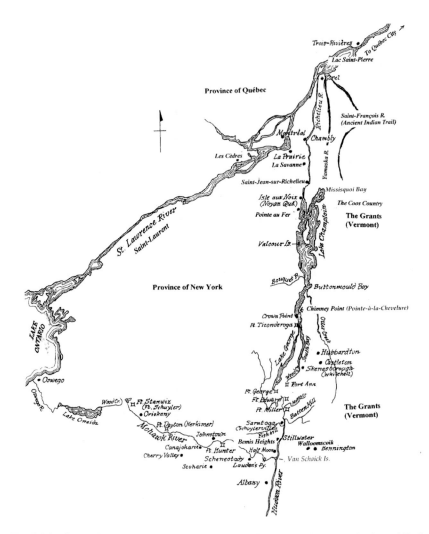

"The Major Sites of the Campaigns of 1776–1777." *Courtesy of Thomas M. Barker and Paul R. Huey,* The 1776–1777 Northern Campaigns of the American War for Independence and Their Sequel: Contemporary Maps of Mainly German Origins (*Fleishmanns, NY: Purple Mountain Press, 2010), frontispiece, 2.*

fight at Hubbardton, Vermont, on July 7. At this point, Burgoyne could have advanced toward Albany and maintained his supply lines to Canada by one of two routes. The first was to recall his army to Ticonderoga and then portage his provisions and guns into Lake George. Burgoyne's army could sail south to Fort George and advance overland to Fort Edward on the Hudson. This route had the advantage of utilizing both Lakes Champlain and George, which would facilitate transportation. Furthermore, because

Fort George was farther south than Skenesborough, the rugged overland trip to Fort Edward was shorter. On the negative side, however, recalling the army to Ticonderoga would take time, a difficult portage connected the lakes and the Americans still held Fort George. Finally, "retreating" to Ticonderoga after having routed the Americans potentially could have hurt British morale and that of the Loyalists who supposedly would join them. Burgoyne's other option was to remain at Skenesborough and march directly to Fort Edward, an action that would place him behind Fort George. This route, however, would necessitate a longer overland march to the Hudson. Burgoyne opted for this second route, and several factors combined to make the difficult twenty-three-mile trek through heavily forested rough terrain even worse.[5]

Burgoyne had not addressed land transportation for his army until early June 1777, when he commissioned horses and carts to transport his artillery and baggage. Burgoyne was unable to procure enough transportation in Canada for all his needs, and he wrongly assumed that he would acquire additional horses and carts as he advanced south. Furthermore, not all the carts and wagons arrived as planned. In fact, his army never had more than 180 carts and 20 or 30 ox carts at one time—in stark contrast to the 500 he had anticipated—and he received only one-third of the horses. The weather complicated Burgoyne's logistical problems, with heavy rains washing out the roads and turning them to mud. The Americans posed the last obstacle by driving away cattle and wagons. They also blocked the roads with fallen trees and destroyed the bridges along the route. As a result, the British advance slowed to a crawl, and Burgoyne did not reach the Hudson until July 29, having covered only twenty-three miles in twenty-one days. Additionally, these transportation and logistical problems made it difficult for the army to accumulate more than one day's provisions at a time.[6]

View of Fort Ticonderoga. *Author's collection.*

Major General Friedrich Riedesel.
Courtesy of the National Archives, 111-SC-92607.

Burgoyne attempted to counter these obstacles in a number of different ways. He dispatched Major General Friedrich Riedesel and some of his Brunswick troops to Castleton, Vermont, to obtain horses and carts, but with only limited success. A number of Loyalists seized sixty cattle near Tinmouth, but in most cases, as one officer reported, "no one would take the risk to surrender or sell the necessary vehicles or horses for the good of our army." Burgoyne also commissioned Philip Skene, a former British officer and prominent local Loyalist, to procure goods and provisions from inhabitants. When none of these efforts proved successful, Burgoyne sought another solution.[7]

Following his return from Castleton, Riedesel had suggested a raid into Vermont to procure horses, especially for his dismounted dragoons. In the face of his growing logistical problems, Burgoyne expanded and adopted the plan on July 31. He selected Lieutenant Colonel Friedrich Baum, a German officer who did not speak English, to command the expedition. Baum was to march toward Manchester and beyond, obtaining provisions and livestock, raising Loyalists for Lieutenant Colonel John Peters's battalion and creating a diversion by threatening the Connecticut River Valley. Skene was to accompany Baum, "in order to assist you, with his advice, to help you to distinguish the good subjects from the bad, [and] to procure the best intelligence of the enemy." Baum's heterogeneous force initially consisted of approximately 760 men: 434 German dragoons and infantry, 200 Loyalists, 50 British marksmen, 60 Canadians and 14 artillerymen with two three-pounder cannons. Around 150 Indians also accompanied the expedition, and they ranged ahead of the main force, alarming the countryside. Burgoyne assigned a number of additional officers to the expedition to provide the interpretative skills necessary to communicate with the English-, German-, French- and Native American–speaking components of Baum's polyglot command. Twenty-four-year-old Lieutenant Desmaretz Durnford, a British engineer who later drew the most detailed map of the battle, also accompanied Baum.[8]

Marker identifying the site of the warehouse that prompted Burgoyne to send Baum to Bennington. The marker stands near the Bennington Battle Monument. *Author's collection.*

While Burgoyne marched through the wilderness and planned Baum's operation, the newly independent state of Vermont, formerly known as the Hampshire Grants, called on New Hampshire and Massachusetts for aid. On July 18, New Hampshire responded by raising three militia regiments, commanded by John Stark, to assist its western neighbor.[9] A former captain in Rogers's Rangers and a veteran of Bunker Hill, Canada, and Trenton, Stark had resigned his Continental army commission in March 1777 after being passed over for promotion. Stark agreed to serve, but only on the condition that he was answerable to New Hampshire, not the Continental army. Large numbers of New Hampshire men quickly enlisted to serve under the legendary Stark, although some were drafted in areas where recruitment lagged. Some soldiers served for economic reasons, such as Alexander Magoon, whose account appears later. Other men served as substitutes for those who were drafted, while still others volunteered because of their belief in the American cause. Overall, Stark had just under 1,500 troops in his brigade, which represented approximately 10 percent of the voting-age men in the state. In some towns, an even larger percentage of males over the age of sixteen served, such as Candia and Salisbury, with 25 and 36 percent, respectively.[10]

The troops began to gather at Fort Number 4, Charlestown, New Hampshire, on the Connecticut River. Stark spent the last week of July and the first one of August organizing his command. He made arrangements for provisions and forwarded soldiers to Manchester as they arrived. He also left one company in Charlestown and sent two others to guard the frontier at Cavendish, Vermont. Having completed his preparations, Stark left for Manchester on August 6. There he conferred with Seth Warner, Colonel William Williams of the Vermont militia and Continental army brigadier general Benjamin Lincoln, who was coordinating militia operations in the region. Stark reiterated his refusal to accept Continental authority but agreed to harass Burgoyne's flank. He and Warner then headed for Bennington, arriving on August 8, where a growing number of his troops and Vermont militia joined them.

Meanwhile, the British army had advanced to Fort Miller, near the Batten Kill, a tributary of the Hudson. Baum set out on his mission from there on August 11. As he left, Burgoyne redirected him to Bennington, rather than Manchester, because intelligence reports indicated that the Americans had collected a large store of provisions and livestock there. Failing to detect Stark, the same reports said that only several hundred militiamen guarded these valuable stores. This was a major change in plans, however, because Baum would now be marching much farther south from Burgoyne's main army rather than roughly perpendicular to it. Riedesel expressed concerns about Burgoyne's changes to his original proposal, but the expedition proceeded.[11] After a short march on August 12, Baum departed early the next morning for

Cambridge, New York. Skirmishing with small detachments of militia and securing a number of livestock, Baum arrived at the village that afternoon, where he also learned of Stark's presence in Bennington.

Resuming his advance on August 14, Baum encountered two hundred of Stark's men near a mill at Sancoick, New York (also known as St. Coick, St. Coix or Rensselaer Mills) about seven miles from Bennington. Lieutenant Colonel William Gregg, the American commander, fired one volley and quickly withdrew, damaging a bridge as he retired. Baum sent a letter to Burgoyne, apprising him of the situation, while his men secured the mill and repaired the bridge. Leaving behind a detachment to protect the mill and gather livestock, Baum continued to march east. Stark, having learned of Baum's presence the night before, requested that Warner's Green Mountain Boys regiment and local militia join him at Bennington. He then marched to support Gregg, who informed him that the enemy was close behind. The two forces made contact along the Walloomsac River about five miles west of Bennington, near a small settlement called Walloomscoick, New York. Stark deployed for battle and tried to induce Baum to attack, but he declined.

Bridge over the Walloomsac River at the Bennington Battlefield. Baum's Canadians manned three cabins on the far side of the river, including one near the house to the left. *Courtesy of Phyllis Chapman.*

Realizing that he faced a larger opponent, Baum ordered his men to entrench and sent a message to Burgoyne, calling for reinforcements. He constructed a breastwork facing northwest atop a steep bluff overlooking the Walloomsac and stationed most of his dragoons and some British marksmen there. At the base of the hill, near the Obediah Beardsley cabin, other Germans defended a smaller breastwork with the two cannons overlooking a bridge. The rest of the British troops manned two small fortifications on the north side of this bridge, while the Canadians occupied several cabins on either side of the span. Several hundred Loyalists built a fieldwork, sometimes referred to as the "Tory Redoubt" or the "Tory Fort," on a small rise on the far side of the Walloomsac.[12] Baum placed other detachments near the dragoon's fortification to protect its right flank, while other troops guarded his baggage and the road on which he had advanced. Overall, his forces were widely scattered and could not support one another if attacked.

A steady stream of Loyalists, many of them unarmed, had joined Baum on the march, and others continued to do so after he arrived at Walloomscoick. Among these was Colonel Francis Pfister, another former British officer and prominent Hoosic, New York Loyalist. A talented engineer, Pfister probably designed and commanded the "Tory Redoubt."[13] These additions brought Baum's command to approximately 1,100, but they also created a serious security problem. Skene foolishly allowed many of the men who entered Baum's camp to take a loyalty oath and then leave with a small card bearing the word "Protection." These cards theoretically identified the bearers as Loyalists. It seems highly likely that some, if not many, of those who entered Baum's position and then left were actually spies working for Stark.

Throughout the campaign, large numbers of civilians, whether they were Whigs, Loyalists or neutrals, fled as Burgoyne's army marched south. They loaded their small children and most valuable possessions onto wagons and livestock, buried those items they were forced to leave behind and sought a safe haven. In some cases, whole families left, but in others, the men remained behind to fight. Ironically, many residents from the Salem (also called New Perth), New York area, such as militiaman Andrew Simson's family, fled to Sancoick, believing that it was out of the path of war. Others went to Bennington itself. As Baum's column advanced, the stream of refugees increased, with many fleeing into Massachusetts. One women later recalled, "I can never forget, while any thing of memory lives, my flight on horseback, and in feeble health, with my babe and two other small children and

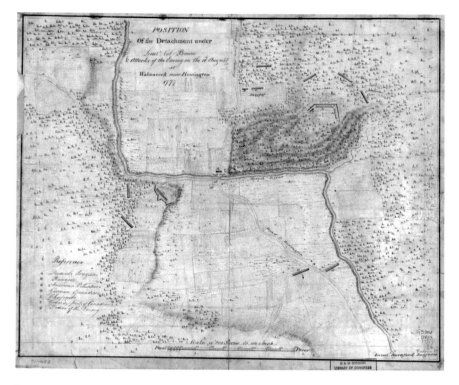

Lieutenant Desmaretz Durnford's map of the Bennington Battlefield. Note that north is the right side of the map. Nichols's and Herrick's attack on the dragoon breastwork atop the high hill is in the top right corner. The Tory Redoubt is located south of the Walloomsac in the left center of the map. Stark's main attack toward the bridge is to the right of this. *Courtesy of the Library of Congress, g3802b ar117700, http://hdl.loc.gov/loc.gmd/g3802b.ar117700.*

my eldest daughter running on foot by the side of me from Bennington to Williamstown under circumstances of great alarm and fear from Hessians, tory-enemies, and Indians."[14]

On August 14 and 15, Vermont, New York and Massachusetts militia, including the Reverend Thomas Allen, whose account of the battle appears later, continued to arrive at Stark's camp several miles west of Bennington. Many of these men formed themselves into makeshift companies. One soldier wrote that "he immediately started for that place [Bennington] where he arrived one or two days before the Battle in company with thirty or forty others and formed themselves into a Company." In another case, a Massachusetts militia captain voluntarily turned over his command to an officer with more combat experience. Although the vast majority of men who fought at Bennington were "amateurs"—that is, not professional soldiers—they did not lack military experience. Some had fought at Bunker Hill, while others participated in the siege of Boston and the invasion of Canada. Most of those who had not seen combat possessed other military service, whether it was garrisoning Ticonderoga, suppressing Loyalists or guarding the frontier. When reading pension records, one cannot help but be struck by the number of times these individuals responded to various alarms, some earlier in the summer of 1777.[15]

By August 15, Stark probably had over two thousand men under his command, with more on the way. He dispatched fifty soldiers to escort cattle to the Continental army, and they were ambushed the following morning in a virtually forgotten engagement that the pension depositions have preserved.[16] Meanwhile, American scouts and spies reconnoitered Baum's position while skirmishers probed his defenses, inflicting thirty casualties. Two important Indian leaders were among those killed. Armed with a steady stream of fresh intelligence and a thorough knowledge of the local area, the American general, with Seth Warner's assistance, spent the day orchestrating an elaborate attack.

Heavy rain fell on August 15, preventing a general engagement, but Stark executed his plan the next day, as he clearly explained: "I sent 300… to oppose the enemy's front to draw their attention that way." Meanwhile, Colonel Samuel Herrick and 300 troops, mainly Vermonters, forded the Walloomsac twice on a long, circuitous trek through the wooded hills to envelop Baum's right rear near the dragoon breastwork. Colonel Moses Nichols led 350 other soldiers on a similar march to encircle Baum's left. Colonels Thomas Stickney and David Hobart advanced toward the Loyalist fortification with 200 men. Once these forces had engaged Baum, Stark would lead his remaining soldiers in an assault on Baum's center near the bridge. Although different colonels led these detachments, considerable intermixing of the American units occurred. Men from New Hampshire, Vermont, New York and Massachusetts served in nearly every detachment. Before dispatching his troops on their various assignments, Stark gave them a short, rousing speech that concluded, "Tonight our flag floats over yonder hill or Molly Stark sleeps a widow."[17] Nichols and Herrick needed time to reach their positions, however, so the attack did not begin until mid-afternoon.

Throughout the day, Baum's scouts detected troops moving into his rear, but he believed that they were Loyalists so paid them little attention. He sent one cannon to the dragoon breastwork on request of its commander but did little else to prepare. Part of Herrick's column became divided and briefly skirmished with a group of Indians, but this failed to rouse the German commander. Meanwhile, Stark's men captured Loyalists attempting to enter Baum's camp. About 3:00 p.m., Nichols's troops opened heavy fire on the dragoon fortification, signaling the attack to begin, and Herrick's men joined in. The Americans traded volleys with the Germans, who also fired the cannon into the nearby forest, trying to keep the attackers at bay. Eventually, the Germans' fire slackened as casualties mounted, and Nichols's and Herrick's soldiers stormed the breastwork on top of the hill. After a short, violent, hand-to-hand struggle, which Joseph Rudd described, the dragoons gave way. One soldier later recalled, "We followed on over their works & pursued down the hill. The day was very warm, they were in full dress & very heavy armed, & we in our shirts & trowses & thus had much the advantage, in the pursuit. Some were killed in their works—Many killed & taken in going down the hill, & others on the flat upon the river." Most of the Indians who had accompanied Baum left the field during this phase of the engagement.

Heavy fighting also took place at the "Tory Redoubt," where Hobart and Stickney led the assault. Massachusetts colonel Joab Stafford discovered a ravine that hid his advance and allowed him to approach the position from behind. As Stafford emerged from the ravine, the Loyalists, surprised to see soldiers in their rear, fired a volley that wounded the colonel in the foot. Hopping on one leg, Stafford urged his men to charge up the side of the hill and into the breastwork. The Loyalists fumbled with their muskets, frantically trying to reload. Meanwhile, other militia, such as Lieutenant John Orr, marched through fields of corn and flax and made a frontal assault against the fortification. Many of the Loyalists were local residents and knew the men who now charged them. Neighbor fought neighbor in fierce hand-to-hand combat, during which Pfister suffered a fatal wound. Struck from both front and rear, the Loyalists broke, just as Baum's other troops had, and fled out the north side of the breastwork.[18] Some of them headed for the bridge while others tried to cross the Walloomsac, with the Americans in hot pursuit.

As the fighting raged on top of the hill and at the "Tory Redoubt," Stark struck Baum's center near the bridge. Quickly routing the Canadians and British soldiers from the cabins and fortifications, his troops stormed across the span and overran the German breastwork overlooking it. There they encountered fugitives from the other parts of the battlefield. The Americans

View of the Walloomsac River. *Courtesy of Phyllis Chapman.*

captured numerous soldiers, including the mortally wounded Baum, along the banks of the Walloomsac, where the Germans attempted a final stand. Interestingly, very few soldiers recounted the fight at the bridge and this final stage of the engagement. Estimates vary on how long the fighting lasted during this first phase of the battle, but it was probably about one hour. Stark's men then scattered. Many were exhausted by the heat and fell out of line. Some scoured the field for prisoners and loot, while Stark sent others back to Bennington with long lines of captives.

The battle was not over yet. After receiving Baum's request for reinforcements, Burgoyne sent Lieutenant Colonel Heinrich Breymann and 642 soldiers toward Bennington on August 15. Heavy rain and mud slowed his approach, and Breymann did not arrive at Sancoick until the following afternoon. He alleged that he had not heard the firing from the first engagement and only learned of Baum's defeat after it was too late to help.[19] Several hundred yards beyond the mill, Breymann came under fire from a group of Americans behind a fence. The German troops easily brushed them aside and deployed for battle, supported by two six-pounder cannons. Resuming the advance, Breymann next encountered a makeshift line that Stark assembled. The German officer later recalled, "Not withstanding fresh support was constantly coming into them, they were driven from every heights. The Troops did their duty and every one concerned, did the same." Just then, Warner's regiment and fresh Massachusetts militiamen led by Major John Rand arrived on the field, stiffening Stark's line.

The two sides battled until sunset in what most participants considered the heaviest fighting of the day and the one that they recorded most fully. The Americans eventually flanked the Germans' left and gained the upper hand. Running low on ammunition, Breymann, wounded in the leg, ordered a retreat. This retreat degenerated into a rout as the Americans pursued. Private Thomas Mellen remembered, "Many of them threw down their guns on the ground, or offered them to us, or kneeled, some in puddles of water." The Germans fled into the growing darkness, and Stark soon halted the pursuit. He later claimed that none would have escaped if night had not fallen. As it was, Stark had won a signal victory. During

Battle of Bennington. *Courtesy of the National Archives, 111-SC-96740.*

the two engagements, the Americans killed 207 enemy soldiers; captured around 700, including 30 officers; and recovered four cannons and a large quantity of military equipment. Estimates of American losses vary, but Stark put the figure at 30 dead and 40 wounded. Over the next several days, Baum's and Breymann's survivors trickled back to Burgoyne's army carrying the news of the disaster.

Burgoyne's prospects had deteriorated dramatically since the heady days of early July when he captured Fort Ticonderoga without a fight. He now found himself alone in the wilderness, short of provisions and awaiting assistance that would never arrive. Although he defeated American militia at Oriskany on August 6, St. Leger eventually retreated to Canada, and the largest part of Howe's army went to Philadelphia instead of advancing up the Hudson. The defeat on the Walloomsac further worsened Burgoyne's plight and marked a turning point in the campaign. It cost him a large number of regular troops, undermined Loyalist support and disheartened the Indians, many of whom returned to Canada soon after the battle. Furthermore, Baum's defeat denied Burgoyne's army the provisions and draft animals that it sorely needed. This forced him to postpone his march south for nearly a month while he gathered supplies, during which time the American army gained strength. Finally, and most importantly, Bennington rejuvenated the colonists' efforts. Prior to the battle, Burgoyne's army moved inexorably toward Albany, overcoming all resistance. Bennington demonstrated that the colonists could win and, in many regards, laid the groundwork for the American victory at Saratoga. Four days after the disaster on the Walloomsac, Burgoyne gloomily apprised the British war minister, Lord George Germain:

> *The great bulk of the country is undoubtedly with the Congress, in principle and in zeal; and their measures are executed with a Secrecy and dispatch that are not to be equaled. Wherever the King's forces point, militia, to the amount of three or four thousand assemble in twenty-four hours; they bring with them their substance & c. &, the alarm over, they return to their farms. The Hampshire Grants in particular, a country unpeopled and almost unknown in the last war, now abounds in the most active and most rebellious race on the continent, and hangs like a gathering storm upon my left.*

BACKGROUND

All the documents retain their original spellings and grammar to give readers a truer feeling for the era.

John Burgoyne's Instructions to Friedrich Baum

Edited a number of times, the following instructions reveal Burgoyne's ambitious plans for Baum's heterogeneous force. Ironically, he strongly cautioned the German officer to protect his command, especially the dragoons. At the last minute, Burgoyne redirected him to Bennington.

> *The object of your expedition is, to try the affections of the country; to disconcert the councils of the enemy, to mount the Reidesel's dragoons, to compleat Peters's corps, and obtain large supplies of cattle, horses, and carriages.*
>
> *The several corps, of which the inclosed is a list, are to be under your command.*
>
> *The troops must take no tents, and what little baggage is carried by officers must be on their own bat horses.*[20]
>
> *You are to proceed from Batten Kill to Arlington, and take post there, till the detachment of the Provincials, under the command of Captain Sherwood, shall join you from the southward.*
>
> *You are then to proceed to Manchester, where you will again take post so as to secure the pass of the mountains on the road from Manchester to Rockingham; from hence you will detach the Indians and light troops to the northward, toward Otter Creek. On their return, and also receiving intelligence that no enemy is in force upon the Connecticut River, you will proceed by the road over the mountains to Rockingham, where you will take post. This will be the most distant part on the expedition.*

General John Burgoyne. *Courtesy of the National Archives, 148-GW-616.*

And must be proceeded upon with caution, as you will have the defile of the mountain behind you, which might make a retreat difficult; you must therefore endeavour to be informed of the force of the enemy's militia in the neighbouring country.

Should you find it may with prudence be effected. You are to remain there while the Indians and light troops are detached up the river. And you are afterwards to descend the River to Brattlebury, and from that place, by the quickest march, you are to return by the great road to Albany.

During your whole progress your detachments are to have orders to bring in to you all horses fit to mount the dragoons under your command, or as to serve as bat horses for the troops, together with as many saddles and bridles as can be found. The number of horses requisite, besides those necessary for mounting the regiment of dragoons, ought to be 1300. If you can bring more for the use of the army it will be so much better.

Your parties are likewise to bring in waggons and other convenient carriages, with as many draft oxen as will be necessary to draw them and all cattle fit for slaughter (milch cows excepted) which are to be left for the use of the inhabitants. Regular receipts, in the form hereto subjoined, are to be given in all places where any of the abovementioned articles are taken, to such persons as have remained in their habitations, and otherwise complied with the terms of General Burgoyne's manifesto; but no receipts to be given to such as are known to be acting in the service of the rebels. As you will have with you persons perfectly acquainted with the abilities of the country, it may perhaps be advisable to tax the several districts with their proportions of the several articles, and limit the hours for their delivery; and should you find it necessary to move before such delivery can be made, hostages of the most respectable people should be taken, to secure their following you the ensuing day. All possible means are to be used to prevent plundering.

As it is probable that Captain Sherwood, who is already detached to the southward, and will join you at Arlington, will drive a considerable quantity of cattle and horses to you, you will therefore send in this cattle to the army, with a proper detachment from Peters's corps, to cover them, in order to disencumber yourself, but you must always keep the regiments of dragoons compact.

The dragoons themselves must ride, and take care of the horses of the regiment. Those Horses which are destined for the use of the army must be tied together by strings of ten each, in order that one man may lead ten horses. You will give the unarmed men of Peters's Corps to conduct them, and the inhabitants whom you can trust. You must always take your camps in a good position; but at the same time where there is pasture, and you must have a chain of centinels around your cattle and horses when grazing.

Colonel Skeene will be with you as much as possible, in order to assist you, with his advice, to help you to distinguish the good subjects from the bad, to procure the best intelligence of the enemy, and to chuse those people who are to bring me the accounts of your progress and success.

When you find it necessary to halt for a day or two, you must always entrench the camp of the regiment of dragoons, in order never to risk an attack or affront from the enemy.

As you will return with the regiment of dragoons mounted, you must always have a detachment of Captain Fraser's or Peters's corps in front of the column, in order to prevent your falling into an ambuscade when you march through the woods.

You will use all possible means to make the country believe that the troops under your command are the advanced corps of the army, and that it is intended to pass to the Connecticut on the road to Boston. You will likewise insinuate that the main army from Albany is to be joined at Springfield by a corps of troops from Rhode Island.

It is highly probable that the corps under Mr. Warner, now supposed to be at Manchester, will retreat before you; but should they, contrary to expectation, be able to collect in great force, and post themselves advantageously, it is left to your discretion to attack them or not, always bearing in mind that your corps is too valuable to let any considerable loss be hazarded on the occasion.

Should any corps be moved from Mr. Arnold's main army, in order to intercept your retreat, you are to take as strong a post as the country will afford, and send the quickest intelligence to me, and you may depend on my making such movements as shall put the enemy between two fires, or otherwise effectually sustain you.

It is imagined the progress of the whole of this expedition may be effected in about a fortnight, but every movement of it must depend on your success in obtaining such supplies of provisions as will enable you to subsist for your return to the army, in case you can get no more. And should not the army be able to reach Albany before your expedition should be compleated, I will find means to send you notice of it, and give your route another direction.

All persons acting in committees, or any officers under the directions of Congress, either civil or military, are to be made prisoners.[21]

Friedrich Baum to John Burgoyne, August 15, 1777

Lieutenant Colonel Friedrich Baum, who commanded Burgoyne's German dragoons, communicated with the British general several times on his ill-fated expedition to Bennington. The following letter, Baum's last, reveals that he faced increased opposition and anticipated the arrival of Breymann's relief column.

Sir,

I HAD the honour of writing to your excellency, and to General Fraser, this morning, at four o'clock, acquainting you to the disposition I had made, as well as of the situation of the enemy, to which I take the liberty of referring; since when I received intelligence from two men who lived on the spot the enemy occupy, it is a strong post which commands a long defile on the road to Bennington: those men declare to have seen yesterday 300 men, who were retreating as my corps advanced, when they were reinforced by 800 men from Bennington. They likewise report we were not a mile distance from the 300 men, when they met with this reinforcement; they mention that all the militia they could get together were at Bennington, and that they expected more to come in, having sent about an hundred miles round for that purpose; many refuse to take arms, wishing to reap their corn and secure their harvest; the inhabitants come in very fast, but want arms. Those accounts have been confirmed by faithful inhabitants sent by Colonel Skeene, who he sent to Bennington, and who fortunately returned.

Your excellency desires to know whether the road is practicable for a large corps with cannon? In consequence I have the satisfaction to inform your excellency that it is good, excepting two or three places which might be rendered equally so by felling a few trees and filling up some holes, which from the constant rain probably have been made worse.

I should be happy to fulfil your excellency's wish as it is a desirable circumstance to be in possession of Bennington; but as the enemy have collected their force, and from their countenance must have had intelligence of ours, would not think it adviseable to risk a repulse, but have secured my post as advantageously as possible; the enemy think Bennington their only resource, as the country around depends on its fate, I therefore will wait your excellency's instructions.

I have read your excellency's orders, relative to the cattle, carts, waggons, flour, wheat, & c. to Colonel Skeene; he is so good as to take this department to himself; and to his honour, has been very active and zealous on this head and in every other respect equally so.

The Bennington Expedition: An Overview

I have communicated to the gentleman commanding the Canadians and Savages, your desire relative to the horses, which they will take particular care to comply with. I have the honour to be most respectfully,
  your excellency's most obedient and humble servant,
F. Baum

Monument marking the house at which Baum and Pfister died on August 18. The monument is located approximately two miles east of the battlefield on the New York–Vermont border. *Author's collection.*

This instant I received a note from Sir Francis, acquainting me that your excellency has been so good to order Lieutenant Colonel Brieman's corps to join.

Mr. Forster, with about ninety volunteers have come in armed, except about thirty; this gentleman is from Hosack.

I beg to repeat to your excellency that the Canadians and Savages want ammunition; and the other volunteers equally want arms.

The enemy have attempted to force our advanced post, but were repulsed on firing the cannon; and at times are throwing up some works about half of a mile.[22]

OVERVIEW OF BATTLE

John Stark

A veteran combat officer from both the French and Indian War and the first two years of the Revolution, Stark choreographed an elaborate attack that overwhelmed Baum's command. In the following letter to the New Hampshire Council, Stark describes his plan, along with the subsequent battle with Breymann, while invoking legendary commanders of the past.

BENNINGTON, August 18, 1777.

GENTLEMAN, I CONGRATULATE you on the late Success of your Troops under my command, by Express, I purpose to give you a brief Account of my Proceedings since I wrote you last.

I left Manchester on the 8th Inst. and arrived here the 9th. The 13th, I was inform'd that a Party of Indians were at Cambridge, which is twelve Miles distant from this Place, on their March thither. I detached Colone Gregg, with two Hundred Men under his command to stop their March. In the Evening I had Information by Express, that there was a lage Body of the Enemy, on their Way, with their Field Pieces, in order to march through the Country, commanded by Governor Skeene. The 14th, I marched with my Brigade, and a few of this State's Militia, to oppose them. and to cover Gregg's Retreat, who found himself unable to withstand their superior Number, about four Miles from this Town, I accordingly met him on his Return, and the Enemy in close pursuit of him, within Half a Mile of his Rear. But when they discover'd me, they presently halted on a very advantageous Piece of Ground; I drew up my little Army on an Eminence, in open View of their

The Bennington Expedition: An Overview

General John Stark. *Courtesy of the National Archives, 148-GW-137.*

Encampments, but could not bring them to an Engagement; I marched back about a Mile, and there encamp'd; I sent out a few Men to skirmish with them, kill'd thirty of them, with two Indian Chiefs. The 15th, It rained all Day; I sent out Parties to harass them. The 16th, I was join'd by this State's militia, and those of Berkshire County. I divided my Army into three Divisions, and sent Col. Nichols with 250 Men on the Rear of their left Wing; Col. Henrich, in the Rear of their Right, with 300 Men, ordered when joined, to attack the same. In the mean Time I sent three Hundred more to oppose the Enemy's Front, to draw their Attention that Way, soon after I detached the Colonels Hubbard and Stickney, on their Right Wing with two Hundred Men to attack that Part, all which Plans had their desir'd Effect, Col. Nichols sent me Word that he stood in need of a Reinforcement, which I readily granted, consisting of one hundred Men, at which Time he commenced the Attack precisely at 3 o'CLOCK, in the Afternoon, which was followed by all the rest, I pushed forward the Remainder with all speed, our People behaved with the greatest Spirit and Bravery imaginable, had they been Alexanders, or Charles's of Sweden, they could not have behaved better; the Action lasted two Hours, at the Expiration of which Time, we forced their Breast works at the Muzzles of their Guns, took two Pieces of Brass Cannon, with a Number of Prisoners, but before I could get them into proper Form again, I received Intelligence, that there was a large Reinforcement within two Miles of us on their march, which occasioned us to renew our Attack, but lucky for us Col. Warner's Regt. came up, which put a stop to their Career, we soon rallied, and a few Minutes the Action began very warm and desperate, which lasted till Night, we us'd their own Cannon against them, which proved *of great Service to us. at Sunset we obliged them to retreat a second Time, we pursued them till dark, when I was obliged to halt for fear of killing my own Men, we recover'd two Pieces more of their Cannon, together with all their Baggage, a number of Horses, Carriages, &c. kill'd upwards of 200 of the Enemy in the Field of Battle, the number of the wounded is not yet known, as they are scatter'd about in many Places. I have one Lieut.- Colonel, since dead, one Major, seven Captains, 14 Lieut's, 4 Ensigns, two Cornets,[23] one Judge Advocate, one Barron, two Canadian Officers, six Serjeants, one Aid de Camp, one Hessian Chaplain, three Hessian Surgeons, and Seven Hundred Prisoners. I inclose you a Copy of Gen. Burgoyne's Instructions to Col. Baum, who commanded the Detachment that engaged us. Our wounded are forty-two; ten Privates & four Officers belonging to my Brigade is dead; the dead and wounded in the other Corps, I do not know, as they have not brought in their Returns as yet.*

I am, Gentlemen, with the greatest Regard and Respect, your most obedient Humble Servant,

JOHN STARKS, Brigadier General.

P.S. I think, we have return'd the Enemy a proper Compliment in the above Action, for the Hubbart-Town Engagement.[24]

One of the three-pounder cannons captured from Baum at Bennington located at the Vermont State Capitol Building in Montpelier. *Author's collection.*

The Bennington Expedition: An Overview

Reverend Thomas Allen

Thomas Allen, a Congregationalist minister from Pittsfield, Massachusetts, was an ardent Whig. Just before the Battle of Bennington, he reputedly called out to the Loyalists in the breastwork and urged them not to fight. He stopped his harangue after one of the defenders shot at him.[25]

Saturday, August 16ᵗʰ, was a memorable day on account of a signal victory the militia under the command of general Starke, obtained over a body of the king's troops commanded by governor Skeene, some account of which is here given by one who was himself in the action. It seems that gen. Burgoyne had detached this corps, consisting of about fifteen hundred men, chiefly Waldeckers and Brunswickers, intermixed with some British troops and Tories, a motley compound, to penetrate as far as Bennington, and farther if it should be found practicable, with a view to increase the number of his friends, to disperse his protections in the country, to procure for his army provisions, and to wreak his wrath and vengeance on those who had disregarded his calls of mercy, and slighted with indignity his proffered protection. Gov. Skeene had advantageously posted his corps within about five miles of Bennington meeting-house, where in different places they made breastworks for their own security. This digression was of such ill tendency, and savoured so much of presumption, that general Starke, who was at that time providentially at Bennington, with his brigade of militia from New-Hampshire state, determined to give him battle. Col. Simond's regiment of militia in Berks county was invited to his assistance; and a part of col. Brown's arrived seasonably to attend on the action, and some volunteers from different towns, and col. Warner with a part of his own regiment joined him the same day. The gen. it seems, wisely laid his plan of operation, and divine providence blessing us with good weather between three and four o'clock P.M. he attacked them in front and flank in three or four different places, at the same instant, with irresistible impetuosity. The action was extremely hot for between one and two hours; the flanking parties had carried their points with greater ease, when the front pressed on to their breastwork with an ardor and patience beyond expectation. The blaze of the guns of the contending parties reached each other, the fire was so extremely hot, and our men easily surmounting their breastworks, amidst peals of thunder and flashes of lightning from their guns, without regarding the roar of their field pieces, that the enemy at once deserted their cover, and ran; and in about five minutes their whole camp was in the utmost confusion and disorder, all their battalions were broken in pieces, and fled most precipitately; at which instant our whole army pressed after with redoubled ardour, pursued them for a mile, made considerable slaughter amongst them, and took many prisoners. One field piece had already fallen into our hands. At this time our men stopped the pursuit, to gain breath, when the enemy being reinforced, our front fell back a few rods for conveniency of ground, and being directed and collected by col. Rasselar, and reinforced by major Stanten, renewed the fight with redoubled ardor, and fell in upon them with great impetuosity, put them to confusion and flight, and pursued them about a mile, making many prisoners, two or three more brass field pieces falling into our hands, and is supposed to be the whole of what they brought out with them. At this time darkness came upon us, and prevented our swallowing up the whole of this body. The enemy fled precipitately the succeeding night towards the North river; and, unless they should be met with by a party of our army there, may have reached there without any farther molestation, Gov. Skeene in surprise and consternation took horse and fled.

This action which redounds so much to the glory of the Great Lord of the Heavens and God of armies, affords the Americans a lasting monument of the divine power and goodness, and a most powerful argument of love to and trust in God. Our loss is about forty or fifty killed, and more wounded. The enemy's loss is greater, and many more wounded. Their baggage fell into our hands. The number of prisoners taken is said to be about six hundred. Two of their colonels were amongst the prisoners, and mortally wounded. A number of inferior officers have also fell into our hands, and in particular the general's aide de camp. A good number deserted and joined us. This victory is thought by some to equal any that has happened during the present controversy; and, as long as prudence, moderation, sobriety, and valor, are of any estimation amongst the United States, will not fail to endear gen. Starke to them. It is the opinion of some, if a large body of militia was now called to act in conjunction with the northern army, the enemy might be intirely overthrown. May all be concerned to give God the glory, whilst we commend the good conduct of the officers and soldiers in general on so important an occasion.[26]

Raising Troops

Alexander Magoon

Alexander Magoon, a private in Captain Chase Taylor's company of Stark's New Hampshire brigade, was in the thick of the fighting at Bennington. After a bullet destroyed the lock on his musket, Magoon picked up a gun from a dead German soldier and continued firing. Later, he staunched the bleeding of a wounded comrade and helped carry his captain back to Bennington when a musket ball shattered his leg. The seventeen-year-old contracted measles soon after the battle and was incapacitated for a month.

That in the Year 1777 in the month of July (as I believe) I was living in the Town of Maultonboro in the State of Newhampshire where there was a call for every fifth man that belonged to the training company to turn out to stop the progress of Burgoynes Army. The Class which I belonged to (the Town being classed into five men to a class) agreed to pay me four dollars pr. month in addition to my wages and I enlisted for two months and was gone several days over three months. Started immediately after my enlistment with a number of others and when we had gotten as far as Sanbornton joined Capt. Taylors Company and marched to Concord where we Joined Col Thomas Stickneys Regiment. From Concord we marched to Charleston (then called number four) from there to Bennington where we arrived a few days before the Bennington Battle.[27]

Benjamin Bean

Private Benjamin Bean of Moultonborough, New Hampshire, had served earlier in the summer of 1777, when he assisted the American forces retreating from Ticonderoga. Like Alexander Magoon, Bean was a private in Captain Chase Taylor's company.

In 1777 the State of New Hampshire was called upon to raise a Brigade of men—John Stark was appointed Brigade General—Capt Ambrose of Mauttenb. was called upon sometime the first part of July to enlist as many men out of his Comp as would be his proportion for the term of two months to march to No 4. accordingly he called his camp and enlisted his quota agreeable to orders—I enlisted and recollect many who served with me…we marched from Mouttenborough the 16ᵗʰ of July and got to Sanburnton the 17ᵗʰ about noon and then passed muster. from there we marched to No. 4, then we drew Rations and each man a lb of powder and balls to go with it—from there we marched to Manchester, there to Bennington where we made a Stand being informed the enemy was coming down from Stillwater—our troops then rallied on Tuesday and we marched 4 miles towards the enemy and then encamped in the open air untill Saturday morning…[28]

Edward Wheeler

Edward Wheeler, a twenty-four-year-old carpenter, moved to Hancock, Berkshire County, Massachusetts, in the spring of 1776 after participating in the siege of Boston with Connecticut troops. Wheeler served at Mount Independence and Fort Ticonderoga in 1776 and 1777 before marching with Captain William Douglas's militia company on the Bennington Alarm.

Citizen-soldier responding to an alarm. *Courtesy of the Granger Collection, New York, Item 0090251.*

That his tour of twelve days in the year 1777 at the time of Bennington Battle was performed at the time of general alarm, when all the militia turned out without distinction or organization until they came to Bennington and were organized for battle, that there was but little discipline among the militia at that time where he was, but at the time of the battle they were mustered and organized in the quickest and easiest manner possible and that he the applicant served as stated in his said declaration. That he was engaged in said battle of Bennington and remained on the field and assisted in burying the dead after the battle.[29]

Amasa Ives

Twenty-nine-year-old Amasa Ives hailed from Adams, Berkshire County, Massachusetts. He first enlisted in 1776, fighting in the New York Campaign. He served again at Bennington in 1777 in Captain Enos Parker's militia company.

His next Service was in the year 1777 at the battle of Bennington, Vermont. He then resided at Adams aforesaid at which time the Country was suddenly alarmed at the approach of the enemy Towards Bennington and a general turning out was the immediate consequence of the alarm, to arrest the progress of the enemy; that this declarant shouldered his musket and repaired the next day to Bennington and the battle was fought the third day after he left home; that he was in the heat of the action, which commenced according to his recollection about 11 O'clock AM and continued till night; that Col. Baum who commanded the enemy received a reinforcement during the action which was the cause of its being continued so long; that the battle was fought as he thinks on the 16th day of August of that year and the enemy completely defeated; that in the battle the company in which this declarant was, was commanded by Enos Parker and the American forces, consisting entirely of militia, were commanded by General Stark…and after the action this declarant returned home after an absence of about one week but this fatigue and excessive heat of the day of the action, caused a severe Sickness which lasted a month or more.[30]

Andrew Simson

Militiaman Andrew Simson resided in Salem, New York, and marched to Ticonderoga in late June with Captain Charles Hutchins's company from Colonel John Williams's regiment. Following the American evacuation of Ticonderoga, Simson's company returned to Salem, where he helped construct a fort and participated in several scouting missions. Baum marched through Sancoick, where the Simson family had fled to keep out of harm's way, and it lay only several miles from the Bennington battleground.

> [T]hat he remained at Salem in said fort until the fore part of August when he was dismissed from said service…and went to his father's who had then removed to a small place twenty miles from Salem called St. Coix; there he remained until the alarm was given that the enemy was in the neighborhood of Bennington a short time after his arrival home and he immediately started for that place where he arrived one or two days before the Battle in company with thirty or forty others and formed themselves into a Company and chose one John Barnes to be their Captain; that the said Company was engaged in the Battle of Bennington and that he was in Said Company at the time and was one of the party under the Command of Col. Herrick who first stormed the breast works of the enemy.[31]

The Battle of Bennington

Description of Battlefield

Bennington Battleground Described

Dr. Asa Fitch (1803–1879), a Salem, New York native, was a physician by training but gained greater renown as both an entomologist and local historian. He interviewed large numbers of people who lived in Washington County during its early settlement and the Revolutionary War.

FITCH'S VISIT

The preceeding sketch is made August 23rd 1850, after having been over the ground August 22nd with U. Barnet Esq. Member of the legislature A.D. 1829—who resides in a brick house where the road crossed the Wallomsac (by a covered bridge 110 feet long) and who owns the ground on which the battle was fought.

Southeast of Esq. Barnet's house across the river a hill arises (clay of hard pan soil) which was cleared at the time of the battle and had a crop of flax pulled and standing in stacks upon the ground. A breast-work was here formed by the enemy, by rails from the adjacent fences, laid up in two tiers parallel with each other and the interstice between filled with this flax. This was the position occupied by the tories at the time of the battle...

There was a bridge across the Wallomsac, at the period of the battle and the road there ran on the same track it now does. This bridge at last rotted

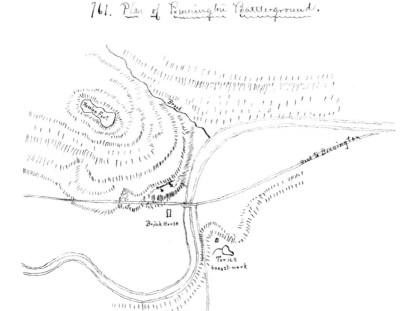

761. Plan of Bennington Battleground.

"Plan of Bennington Battleground." This map is oriented with the north on the top of the map. The Barnet House is located in the middle of the map, north of the Walloomsac. *Courtesy of Saratoga National Historical Park, Asa Fitch Letterbook, SARA 4136, Item 761.*

down and for many years the river was forded here till the present covered bridge was built.

North of the road, on the west side of the river is an abrupt rise of slate rock nearly a precipice—and a height of some 60 feet or a 100 above the river is a flattish level of small extent, above the steep rise. Here two cannon of Baum stood at the time of the battle. Baum supposed Stark would come down along the highway from Bennington and attack the tories breastwork first, and the cannons were placed here to give him a raking fire as he came. The position overlooking the flat above. But Stark kept in the north side of the stream wholly out of sight and reach of the cannon, as Esq. B. has always understood, and followed up the hollow in which the brook runs till he came directly upon the Hessian breastwork, with his whole forces. And the party that attacked the tory breastwork came around from the east into its rear, so that the cannon could not play upon them without killing the tories, whose position was between the cannon and the assailants as they advanced. Thus the cannon did the enemy very little if any service, upon the day of the battle...

FORT ON THE HILL WHERE THE MAIN BATTLE WAS FOUGHT

The hill north of the road and north of U. Barnet's house, rises with a gentle ascent—being ledgy in many places and with but a slight covering of soil over the rock which is slate. It has many hummocks and irregularities, adapting it well for defense especially when covered with forest trees. It rises to a height of some 500 feet above the river and its summit is about 140 rods[32] or ½ mile from the bridge...There is a small level spot on its summit, some 12 rods long and a third as wide, where the Hessians made their stronghold. The hill was covered with the forest at that time. Here upon the summit the trees were cut away and thrown into a timber breastwork—there not being soil enough to admit of making a ditch or embankment—and not the faintest vestige of the breastwork is now visible. They enclosed themselves on all sides, it is believed their work being a fort rather than a breastwork. A single oak tree was left standing within the enclosure, perhaps to suspend their colors from, it being nearly impossible to dig a hole here to plant a flag-staff. This tree has long been

View of the Bennington Battlefield circa 1900 from the Tory Redoubt (10). The location of the dragoon breastwork is visible atop the hill (6) across the Walloomsac. The breastwork with cannons (8) overlooked the bridge, while the Canadians manned cabins on the near side of the river (9). *Author's collection.*

The Barnet House on the Bennington Battlefield. The bridge over the Walloomsac River is to the right. The Obediah Beardsley cabin stood in the right background, and the German breastwork overlooking it was on the hill behind the pine tree. *Courtesy of Phyllis Chapman.*

dead, the stump only remaining uprooted and far decayed...The level top of the hill runs in a N.W. and S.E. direction and descends on all sides—but to the N.W. the descent is but slight and the ridge continuing ¾ of a mile shoots up into a still higher point called Cobble hill across which the county boundary line runs.

The hill was entirely cleared up after the war, and is now covered with a grove of second growth trees which have now been growing 28 years. The flats along the river were all cleared at the time of the battle and in places the clearing reached up into the hills. A house stood some rods S.W. of where the brick house now stands and there were several log huts in the neighborhood—the land there being held mostly under leases of 21 years duration—no good houses had been built.

About 40 rods north of the Hessian fort Esq. Barnet in plowing ten years ago picked up a lead bullet in the direction in which Stark advanced. This he presented me for the State Antiquarian Collection. Balls and other relics of the battle used to be often found but they are all scattered and lost, and nothing of the kind is met with any more, the land has been so much plowed.[33]

Gregg's Skirmish

William Gilmore of Cambridge and a few other, stripped the plank of the bridge at San Coick (North Hoosic) as Baum approached but Baum was too near upon them to enable them to cut the string pieced and let them down into the water. (This appears to have been the first decidedly hostile stop Baum met with on his march.) And whilst they were repairing the bridge one man and another was firing upon them from bushes and other coverts.[34]

Samuel Eaton

Private Samuel Eaton, nineteen, served two tours of duty in the summer of 1777. Following the battle, he was one of the thirty soldiers who escorted the captured stores to Albany.

In June 1777, started for Ticonderoga under Capt. Joshua Martin and marched as far as Washington, New Hampshire and there received orders that we were not wanted and returned home, was absent about ten days. A few days after arriving home at Goffstown, declarent was warned to a training and was there drafted and immediately marched to Charlestown (No. 4) stayed there about one week from there marched to Manchester, VT under command of Capt. McConnell, stopped there about one week and then marched for Bennington. Arrived there

Monument marking Gregg's skirmish at Sancoick Bridge. *Author's collection.*

on Sunday, and on Monday was called out on a Scout under Col. Graigue and marched to Rainlow Mills, N. York, twelve miles from Bennington and there made a Stand. And took up the Bridge to prevent the Enemy from crossing but the project failed, and we then retreated back to Bennington, where we met General Stark with the main Army and then made a Stand for a few days.[35]

NICHOLS'S ATTACK

John Austin

Private John Austin, twenty-three, served in Captain Samuel McConnell's company in Colonel Thomas Stickney's New Hampshire militia regiment. In addition to providing a view of the battle, Austin's account also reveals the mixing of military units that occurred on the American side, as he fought with Colonel Moses Nichols.

I was drafted in the N. Hampshire militia of infantry for two months as a private. we marched for Burgoine's Army and reached Bennington Vt. where we joined Gen. Stark and his forces and we were in the Bennington Battle. The British had a detachment with one field piece stationed about half a mile from their main body which had thrown up an entrenchment—I was one of a detachment of one hundred men ordered under the command of Colos. Nichols and Reed to march round through the woods in the rear of this detachment of the British and dislodge them or also by so doing to divert the attention of the main British force from the advance of our main body and were ordered to fire which should be the signal for this action to begin with our main body. we affected our motion in the rear of the British detachment and first sent forward several scouts which each returned bringing in little squads of tories who were going in to the British having pieces of white paper of the size of a card stuck on their hats having wrote thereon "Protection." we then advanced and fired. the main army in a moment fired also. we rushed on, drove the British detachment from their entrenchments and went in upon their main body—we drove the enemy till in their retreat they met a reinforcement.[36]

This spotted hawthorn tree (*Crataegus punctata*), the largest in New York, stands on the Bennington Battlefield near where Herrick's and Nichols's men assembled before attacking the dragoon breastwork. *Author's collection.*

John Meriam Jr.

Twenty-year-old John Meriam Jr. served as Captain Christopher Webber's waiter in Colonel David Hobart's New Hampshire militia regiment during the Bennington campaign. Many veterans such as Meriam sought out statements from fellow soldiers, family and friends to support their pension applications.

> [I] *say that in the year 1777 I was in the northern army on the two month service at and near Bennington and in the Bennington Battle. And that while there I saw John Meriam...that he was then doing duty as a private in the same Regiment that I was Col Nichols—tho not in the same Company. Saw him in Bennington. Saw him soon after his return; had conversation with him about the battle; had a pair of Hessian gaiters on him which he informed me he brot home with him; and understood from him then, that he passed over the Hessian breast work among the first and showed me several holes in his clothes which he then said were made by musket balls in that action.*
> Asa Wilcox   July 13, 1832[37]

Jesse Bailey

Like John Meriam Jr., Jesse Bailey also served in Webber's company, and like John Austin, he assisted in capturing Loyalists who were on their way to join Baum.

> *That he marched from Charlestown to Manchester in Vermont and then to Bennington where he arrived the Wednesday previous to the battle that he was in that battle and was in the diversion which Genl. Stark (commander in the engagement) sent on to the right of the Enemy to commence the attack and thinks he was among the first who fired in that engagement. He recollects that just before the action commenced he assisted in taking ten tories who were coming to join the Enemy; that he disarmed and took two Hessians during the action. He and his Lieutenant was a little in advance of the main body of our army when the reinforcement to the British Army came up and was the first who fired upon the reinforcing troops.*[38]

HERRICK'S ATTACK

Jesse Field

Like Dr. Asa Fitch, future Vermont governor Hiland Hall (1795–1885) possessed a great interest in local history. He interviewed a number of Bennington residents who had fought in the famous battle. Jesse Field, who served in the Bennington militia, is the first of these interviews reprinted in this book.

I Jesse Field…say that previous to, [and] at the time [of]…the battle of the 16th of August '77 I had resided in Bennington. Previous to the battle some barracks & store houses had been erected in Bennington by the Govt. of Vermont, in which a quantity of provisions was deposited, & I think some had been brought from Berkshire Co. Mass—the quantity of stores I am not able to tell, but should think it was not large. Genl Stark arrived in town 4 or 5 days previous to the 16th—A few days before the battle say the 12th or 13th the scouts brought information that a body of Hessians tories & Indians were approaching Bennington & were with 12 or 15 miles of the town. On the 14th Stark marched in the direction of the enemy & sent a party in advance who met Baum near Rensalaer's Mills & retreated. I cannot tell exactly how far Stark advanced with the main body that day but he encamped on the farm now owned by David Henry.

The 15th was a rainy day & the main body remained in camp. Scouting parties were, however, out all day & there was some skirmishing, but I am not able to give the particulars. I belonged to Capt Dewey's company of militia. On the morning of the 16th a body of troops was detached to attack the enemy on the north, & Col Herrick with his regiment of rangers & a part or the whole of Col. Brush's regiment of Militia including Capt Dewey & Cap. Saml Robinson's company of militia from Bennington crossed the river nearby agt. [against] the camp went over the hills & forded the river again below the enemy & came up in their rear from the south west. I was on or near the right & front of the party—When we came in sight of the works we halted, & it seemed that the rear of our party had been detained for some cause & did not come on so quick as they ought to have done—We stood but a short time when the firing commenced from the party on the north. I recollected of hearing Lieut. [blank] exclaim—"My God what are we doing—they are killing our brothers—Why are we not ordered to fire"—In a moment our adjutant rode up & ordered us to advance—We pressed forward & as the Hessians rose

The dragoon breastwork stood approximately where the monuments are. Herrick's and Nichols's men approached the position from the left and right rear, respectively, through the trees in the background. *Author's collection.*

above their works to fire we discharged our pieces at them, we kept advancing & about the 2nd fire they left their works & ran down the hill to the south or S. East—We followed on over their works & pursued down the hill. The day was very warm, they were in full dress & very heavy armed, & we in our shirts & trowses & thus had much the advantage, in the pursuit.

Some were killed in their works—Many killed & taken in going down the hill, & others on the flat upon the river. After we passed the redoubt there was no regular battle—all was confusion, a party of our men would attack & kill or take prisoners another party of Hessians—Every man seemed to manage for himself & being attached by chance to a squad either under some leader or without any would attack any party that come in their way—In this way the pursuit was continued until they were all or nearly all killed or taken. I should think I did not pursue more than ½ a mile tho' some parties went further, probably nearly or quite down to the mills...When the prisoners were collected, they were sent off under a guard to Bennington. Our men were then scattered all over the field of battle, some resting & refreshing themselves, some looking up the dead & wounded, & others in pursuit of plunder...

In the first battle the party under Nichols might have commenced the attack two minutes before us & from the time we commenced until we entered the works it might have been five minutes, tho I think it was nearer two—It seemed but an instant—They appeared pannick struck at our first fire—ran over their works down the hill & we after them—There was firing after wards, tho' irregular & principally by our men to prevent their escape—Such is my impression.[39]

Silas Walbridge

Another veteran interviewed by Hiland Hall, Silas Walbridge served in Samuel Herrick's Vermont Rangers.

Silas Walbridge of Bennington says that he was at the evacuation of Ty. & in hearing of the battle of Hubbardton, but the Genl would not suffer the men to return—that at Pawlet (34 miles from B.) he saw Captn. John Warner (brother of Col. W) who informed him that the Govt of Vt. were raising a Regt of Rangers for 6 mo. to be commanded by Col Herrick, & that he then enlisted under him—that Capn Warner & himself came on to Manchester & remained there recruiting until the 15th of Augt when Capt W rcd a letter calling him to B. that they arrived at Ben. that evening—& found the Regt at Stark's encampment early in the morning as the troops were parading for battle—that Herrick's Regt consisting of 4 companies, perhaps 200 men together with Brush's Regt of Militia—or a part of them, the Bengton & Pownal men certainly—went from the encampment west across the river, crossed it again below R [Rensselaer] Mills & came in in the rear of the Hessian redoubt—that just before they arrived at the redoubt they came in sight of a body of Indians & fired on them—they retreated to the N. West leaving two killed—

Our men came within ten or twelve rods of the redoubt & began firing from behind logs trees & c. & continued occasionally advancing until the Hessians retreated out of their works down the hill to the south. Nichol's men began firing ahead of the time we did & the action was short from 15 to 20 or possibly 30 minutes.—We followed on down the hill on to the flat, & I afterwards with Capt Warner went back to where the battle began to look for the wounded. While there we heard firing the beginning of the second battle...[40]

Joseph Rudd

Joseph Rudd, thirty-seven, served as a lieutenant in Captain Elijah Dewey's Bennington militia company. In later years, he participated in events commemorating the battle.

Mr. Rudd related to me that he carried his sword and gun into the battle of Bennington, that after with others had stormed the breastwork, and the Hessians were retreating and firing, he snapped his gun at a stout built Hessian, and that from some cause, and for the first time on that day his gun missed fire, that he pursued to grapple with the Hessian to take him a prisoner. The Hessian turned and raised his piece to fire, but Mr. Rudd said he was so near to him that by a spring and quick effort he knocked the Hessian's gun up, and he grappled with him drew the Hessian's sword instead of his own, and gave the Hessian a severe blow on his neck as he broke from him and turned to run. And that Mr. Herrick struck the Hessian with the

One of Baum's Dragoons. *Courtesy of the Bennington Museum, Bennington, Vermont, Item A4224.*

but of his gun and killed him. Mr. Rudd said he always regretted Herrick's killing the Hessian for he meant to have brought him in as a prisoner. The sword Mr. Rudd took from the Hessian I have seen. I have also heard Mr. Herrick and others relate repeatedly the same story.
Amos Searles[11]

"Tory Redoubt"

John Orr

Lieutenant John Orr, of Samuel McConnell's company, provides one of the most vivid and complete accounts of the fighting at the "Tory Redoubt."

I was in a detachment of 200, to attack the minor breastwork...We marched from the main body, about half a mile, and then arranged ourselves in front of the breast-work about fifty or sixty rods distant, with trees and corn intervening, which prevented our seeing each other.

About 4 o'clock, P.M., Nichols began, and the cracking of muskets was such, that imagination could see men falling by dozens. We arose and with shouts marched rapidly to the attack. In the meantime, I remembered the fate of Col. Hale, who, about two months before, was overtaken in his retreat from Ticonderoga, by the enemy, skulked in the beginning of the action, lost his standard, and was degraded. Resolving that no one should have cause to impeach me with cowardice, I marched on with the appearance of a brave soldier. When we had passed through the wood and cornfield, we came in sight of the enemy, at about fifteen rods distance. They commenced firing with muskets, at an alarming rate, so that it seemed wonderful that any of the attacking party should escape. At that time, an expression of the Prince of Orange came into my mind, "every bullet has its billet," and I soon found one commissioned to lay me low. After having lain fifteen or twenty minutes, one of our sergeants came and offered to take me off the ground, I told him he was unable, for I could not help myself. He said he would not leave me there, for the enemy might come and kill me. He therefore called a soldier to his assistance. They took hold of me by my arms, and attempted to carry me off; but the balls flew directly at us, so that I charged them to lay me down instantly, each take a hand, and stoop so low, that the flax would conceal them, and drag me on my back, into the cornfield, where I should be out of sight of the enemy. This order they obeyed, and took me to the road, where many of the wounded were collected. I was then carried to the General's quarters, where I lodged that night without rest.[42]

Joab Stafford

Forty-seven-year-old Colonel Joab Stafford led a company of independent volunteers from New Providence (modern-day Cheshire), Massachusetts. His son provided the following account many years later.

When they reached the ground, they found the Hessians posted in a line; and on a spot of high ground, a small redoubt was seen formed of earth just thrown up, where they understood a body of loyalists or provincial troops, that is, tories, was stationed. Colonel Warner had command under

A view of the ravine through which Stafford's men marched to attack the Tory Redoubt from behind. The photograph, taken in mid-summer, reveals the thickness of the vegetation. Note the ravine's steep slope and the view of the road on the left top onto which Stafford emerged. *Courtesy of Phyllis Chapman.*

General Stark; and it is generally thought that he had more to do than his superior in the business of the day. He was held in high regard by the Massachusetts people; and my father soon reported himself to him, and told him he awaited his orders. He was soon assigned a place in the line, and the tory fort was pointed out as his particular object of attack.

There was an aged and excellent old man present, of a slender frame, stooping a little with advanced age and hard work, with a wrinkled face, and well known as one of the oldest persons in our town, and the oldest on the ground. My father was struck with regard for his aged frame, and, much as he felt numbers to be desirable in the impending struggle, he felt a great reluctance at the thought of leading him into it. He therefore turned to him, and said: "The labors of the day threaten to be severe, it is therefore my particular request, that you will take your post as a sentinel yonder, and keep charge of the baggage." The old man stepped forward with an unexpected spring, his face was lighted up with a smile, and pulling off his hat, in the excitement of his spirit, half affecting the gayety of a youth, while his loose hair shone as white as silver, he briskly replied: "Not till I've had a shot at them first, captain, if you please." All thoughts were now directed towards the enemy's line; and the company, partaking in the enthusiasm of the old man, gave three cheers. My father was set at ease again in a moment; and orders being soon brought to advance, he placed himself at their head, and gave the word: "Forward, march!"

He had observed some irregularity in the ground before them, which he had thought might favor his approach; and he soon discovered that a small ravine, which they soon entered, would cover his determined little band from the shot of the enemy, and even from their observation, at least for some distance. He pursued its course; but was so far disappointed in his expectations, that, instead of terminating at a distance from the enemy's line, on emerging from it, and looking about to see where he was, he found the fresh embankment of the tory fort just above him, and the heads of the tories peeping over, with their guns leveled at him. Turning to call on his

The rise upon which the Tory Redoubt stood, seen from Stafford's perspective as he emerged from the ravine. *Courtesy of Phyllis Chapman.*

men, he was surprised to find himself flat on the ground without knowing why; for the enemy had fired, and a ball had gone through his foot into the ground, cutting some of the sinews just as he was stepping on it, so as to bring him down. At the same time, the shock had deafened him to the reports of the muskets.

The foremost of his soldiers ran up and stooped to take him in their arms, believing him to be dead or mortally wounded; but he was too quick for them, and sprang on his feet, glad to find he was not seriously hurt, and was able to stand. He feared that his fall might check his followers; and, as he caught a glimpse of a man in a red coat running across a distant field, he cried out, "Come on, my boys! They run! They run!" So saying, he sprang up, and clambering to the top of the fort, while the enemy were hurrying their powder into the pans and the muzzles of their pieces, his men rushed upon the defenders so closely, that they threw themselves over the opposite wall, and ran down the hill as fast as their legs would carry them.[43]

Pardon Mason

Pardon Mason, of Cheshire, Massachusetts, served two tours of duty in 1776. Two days past his nineteenth birthday, he was reputedly the second man over the breastwork when the Americans stormed the "Tory Redoubt."

[T]hat after they had arrived at Bennington…he was again put in the Company of said Daniel Brown and at the battle was put into a flanking party under Col. Stafford. we attacked a flanking party of the enemy in which attack Col. Stafford was wounded in his ankle by Musket ball, which deprived him of the use of one foot but notwithstanding this he hopped upon one foot, with the help of his musket and attacked a Breastwork which the party Stormed and took.[44]

Joseph Clark

Corporal Joseph Clark and his brother, Edward, served in Captain Jeremiah Post's company in Colonel David Hobart's New Hampshire militia regiment. Joseph was promoted to sergeant after the battle, but both he and his brother developed the "camp disorder" and were sent home.

That in the Summer of 1777...the town of Haverhill was called on for ten men to go over the green mountains and fight the British. That he was drafted and immediately marched under Capt. Post of Oxford to No. 4 now Charlestown where they halted some days and then marched to Bennington in Vermont and was stationed there to guard stores. That he was in the battle with the British who came up to take the stores. That Capt. Post was wounded and disabled in the battle and died in a few days afterwards. That Capt. Post called on him to carry him off the ground. That he refused at first. That Capt. Post then said "For God's sakes don't let me fall into their hands alive!" That he (Clark) spoke to the sergeant major and they together carried him to a house where he died. That the American army was drawn up in front of the enemy's breast works. That a hundred men were ordered into the rear of the enemy (these were taken from the right wing). That another hundred were taken from the left wing and posted behind a fence and ordered to rush on as soon as the first hundred began the battle. That he was one of the hundred from the left and heard the order given by Genl. Stark himself.[45]

Diversion in the Center

Nathan Mason

Nathan Mason, twenty-one, resided in Lanesborough, Berkshire County, Massachusetts. In July 1777, he marched to Manchester and assisted Colonel Seth Warner's Green Mountain Boys regiment following the Battle of Hubbardton. Mason returned home approximately one month later and immediately volunteered to serve again, this time at Bennington.

[I]n the Month of August he Volunteered to enter a draft for three months and entered the service...and within two hours he was marched from Lanesborough and marched through the town of Adams—Williamstown—Pownal into Bennington where he Joined Col. Simmons Regiment which was commanded by Lieut. Col. Powel. The Col being Lame and indisposed. Gen. Stark commanded the troops. he was marched to the attack of Col. Baum who lay with his men in his entrenchments about seven miles from Bennington and he encamped within half a mile from Baum behind a hill which rise of Ground was between them and on Sixteenth day of August before the sun rose he was marched to the top of the hill in Sight of the enemy, remained

there a short time and was Marched back to camp and eat his breakfast with all the men and after breakfast Col. Herrick he thinks came In front of his Regiment and requested three hundred Volunteers who turned out and Marched away soon after. Col. Stickney he thinks came also in front of his Regiment once Requested three hundred Volunteers who turned out and likewise marched away during this time. Gen. Stark marched past with his Brigade. this declarent was then Marched by Major Stastten and Adjutant Stone to the top of the hill and there were a few Scattering shots exchanged and the enemy fired upon them with their Artillery. during this time this declarent has reason to believe that the Americans were making necessary arrangements to attack the enemy in the rear for at 3 O'Clock in the afternoon the main action commenced on the left wing of Baums intrenchments and in his rear at which time he was marched in the front of Baums troops and commenced a fire upon the enemy and they were killed and taken prisoners. That Col. Baum was wounded and died of his wounds and that Col. Fister who commanded the Indians and Tories was also wounded and died and he this declarent see Fister expire.[46]

FIGHT WITH BREYMANN

Jesse Field

Perhaps an hour before sunset I heard the report of cannon, & news soon came that we were attacked by a body of Hessians, who had come to reenforce Baum—We went down upon the side hill north of the road—The Hessians were marching up the road, their cannon in front, clearing the way—Our men kept collecting in front, & on the right—Our party were on the side hill within from 12 to 20 rods from them generally behind trees & kept up a constant fire the road appeared full of men & it was like firing into a flock of sheep—They kept firing but with very little success. The battle continued until dusk when they retreated, & were not pursued far—My position was such during in this engagement that I am not able to give any further account of it, nor relate the part which Warners regiment acted, tho' I have no doubt we were greatly indebted to them for our success...I have always thought the 2ⁿᵈ to be the longest & hardest fought action.[47]

Thomas Mellen

Thomas Mellen served as a private in Captain Peter Clark's company of New Hampshire militia in Colonel Thomas Stickney's regiment.

[W]*e met Breymann with eight hundred fresh troops and larger cannon, which opened a fire of grape shot. Some of the grape shot riddled a Virginia fence near me, one struck a small white oak tree behind which I stood. Though it hit higher than my head, I fled from the tree, thinking it might be aimed at again. We skirmishers ran back, till we met a large body of Stark's men, then faced about. I soon started for a brook I saw a few rods behind, for I had drank nothing all day, and should have died with thirst had I not chewed a bullet all the time. I had not gone a rod when I was stopped by an officer, sword in hand, and ready to cut me down as a runaway. On my complaining of thirst, he handed me his canteen, which was full of rum. I drank and forgot my thirst.*

But the enemy outflanked us, and I said to a comrade: "We must run or they will have us." He said: "I will have one more fire first." At that moment a major on a black horse rode along behind us, shouting: "Fight on, boys; reinforcements close by." While he was yet speaking, a grape shot went through his horse's head, and knocked out two teeth. It bled a good deal, but the major kept his seat, and spurred on to encourage others. In five minutes we saw Warner's men hurrying to help us. They opened right and left of us, and half of them attacked each flank of the enemy, and beat back those who were just closing around us. Stark's men now took heart and stood their ground. My gun-barrel was by this time too hot to hold, so I seized the musket of a dead Hessian, in which my bullets went down easier than in my own. Right in front were the cannon, and seeing an officer on horseback waving his sword to the artillerymen, I fired at him twice. The horse fell. He cut the traces of an artillery horse, mounted him, and rode off. I afterwards heard that the officer was Major Skene.

Soon the Germans ran, and we followed. Many of them threw down their guns on the ground, or offered them to us, or kneeled, some in puddles of water. One said to me: "Wir sind ein, bruder!" ["We are one, brother!"] *I pushed him behind me and rushed on. All those near me did so. The enemy beat a parley, minded to give up, but our men did not understand it. I came to one wounded man, flat on the ground, crying water, or quarter. I snatched his sword out of his scabbard, and, while I ran on and fired, carried it in my mouth, thinking I might need it. The Germans fled by the road, and in a wood each side of it. Many of their scabbards caught in the brush, and held the fugitives till we seized them. We chased them till dark. Colonel Johnson, of Haverhill, wanted to chase them all night. Had we done so, we might have mastered them all, for they stopped within three miles of the battle-field. But Stark, saying he would run no risk of spoiling a good day's work, ordered a halt and return to quarters…*

My company lay down and slept in a cornfield near where we had fought; each man having a hill of corn for a pillow. When I waked next morning, I was so beaten out that I could not get up till I rolled about a good while.[48]

Thomas Farnsworth

Following the Battle of Lexington in April 1775, Minuteman Thomas Farnsworth, of Westminster, Massachusetts, marched to Cambridge, where he subsequently enlisted for eight months. In 1776 and 1777, he served as a substitute for other men who had been drafted. In the latter case, he served in Captain John Joslin's militia company in Colonel Job Cushing's regiment during the Bennington Alarm.

[W]*hen I marched to Bennington Maj. Rand had the command…Maj. Rand's horse was shot through the nose and dock.*[49] *I was his waiter and with him in the action. Genl Stark had the chief command, Col Warner, Col Bill Williams was there. After the Battle of Bennington was over I asked permission to go on to the battleground, and Maj. Rand told me to go, and take his canteen and go to Brother Williams and get it filled with rum, Maj. Rand and Williams were Brothers-in-laws.*[50]

Jacob Safford

Jacob Safford, another Bennington veteran whom Hiland Hall interviewed, served as an orderly sergeant in Colonel Seth Warner's Green Mountain Boys regiment.

After the battle of Hubbardton, by which our regt. was reduced to less than 200 men, we were stationed at Manchester. On the 14th of August, I should think, information was received that we were wanted at Bennington; but owing to the absence of a large scout under Capt. John Chipman & perhaps from some other causes, we did not march till the morning of the 15th. The day was rainy, but by marching till nearly midnight we arrived within about a mile of Bennington village & encamped. We were drenched with rain, & our arms & equipment having been all day exposed to the weather, it took a considerable part of the forenoon of the next day to fit ourselves for a march.

We were also short of ammunition which occasioned some delay & so much time was employed in making the necessary preparations for battle, that it was about noon or perhaps a little past, when the regt. marched from Bennington village. While going down the Henderson hill (2 miles from B) a scattering fire of musketry was commenced in the direction of the battle ground. We halted a short time at Stark's encampment (4 miles from B) left our coats & knapsacks, & a gill of rum with water was dealt to each man. The weather was extremely warm, & after crossing the first bridge (about 5¾ miles from B) we were halted while the men drank at the river. Two sergeants were now requested to volunteer to head the lines, & I with another went in front. About this time the firing, which had gradually increased, became very heavy, & a general attack seemed to be made. We now began to meet the wounded & when we arrived at the second bridge (3/4 of a mile below the first) the Hessians were running down the hill & the two pieces of cannon were taken.

If we halted at all at this place, it was but for a very few minutes. Here I was first in command of the left flank guard, & the march was continued by the regt. down the road, & by myself & guard across the flat. There was also a flank guard on the right. We continued our march until we came to the top of the eminence next beyond where the brick factory now stands (1½ miles below the 2nd bridge) where I found the regt. had halted. On inquiring the cause I was told that a reinforcement of the enemy was near. I mounted a fence & saw the enemy's flank guard beyond the next hill, say half a mile distant. We were then ordered to form a line for battle by filing to the right, but owing to the order not being understood in the rear the line was forward by filing to the left, which brought many of our men into a sort of swamp instead of on the hill above, where we should have been. We however waited the approach of the enemy & commenced firing as they came up, but owing, as I think, to the unfavorable nature of the ground we soon began a retreat, which was continued slowly & in good order firing constantly, for about ¾ of a mile until we reached the high ground west of the run of water, where we made a stand.

The enemy had two pieces of cannon in the road, & their line extended a considerable distance both below & above the road. A party of Hessians undertook to out flank us on the right, & partly succeeded, but were finally repulsed & driven back. The action was warm & close for nearly two hours, when, it being near dark the enemy were forced to retreat. One of their pieces of cannon was taken near the run, & the other a few rods below the brick factory.

I should think the scatting fire continued an hour & a half before the first action had become general, & that after it became general, it lasted from 15 to 30 minutes.

Col. Warner's regiment was marched from Manchester under the command of Maj. Saml Safford. Col. Warner had been at Bennington for several days before the battle, & I have always understood was very serviceable to Genl Stark in planning & managing the first, as well as the second action.[51]

Nathan Mason

That after the battle with Baum he with some others pursued after those that had fled further [?] expected and come upon the reinforcement commanded by Col Brickman but did not discover them until they fired upon them or him with canister Shot which went over his head. he then retreated he thinks half a mile when he met his Regiment and Joined them and fought on the retreat until a line of battle was formed at which time Col. Warner came up with his continental Regiment and then the action was Sustained after which Col. Brickman was compelled to retire. the firing continued however until dark after which the Enemy went away under the cover of the night. That there were about three hundred taken prisoners; Brickman was wounded in his ankle and leg during the action. That after the dead were buried and on Monday following he was marched to the Village of Bennington where the Prisoners were and he was elected as one of the guard to take charge of them.[52]

Second Battle of Bennington

Dr. Asa Fitch recorded the following account of the battle with Breymann's column.

Rueben Clark says, as he has always been told the second engagement was as follows:

When Baum was defeated on the hill north of Barnets, the fugitives that escaped from being captured fled back and were pursued by the Americans in an irregular manner and without any order. They passed through the Wallomsac settlement...which is 1½ miles from Barnet's house. About on the west line of Wallomsac patent...a ledge of rock crosses the valley—extending from the hill which bounds this valley from the north, down towards the Wallomsac river, forming a ridge some 10 feet about the level plain west of it and having some brooks and slight ravines on its east side. The flying Hessians as they gained this ridge (pursued by the Americans) to their great relief saw Breyman advancing on the flat beyond them. The road then ran north of where it does now, on the north side of the flat near the base of the hill. The Hessians ran on and joined their friends and the pursuing Americans, on gaining the summit of the ridge and seeing the imposing force in front of them, they paused and fired upon it till Breyman had arranged his men for advancing—his two cannon charged with grape shot, were fired sending much showers of balls that the Americans forsook the ridge and took to the ravines and bushes in its rear. This was only an irregular force of Americans, without order in their ranks or a general officer to direct their movements—most of the American force being scatted about various parts of the battlefield, securing horses or any other plunder they could find.

Breyman's forces advanced, passed over the ridge, the scattered Americans retiring before them, a desultory firing only was kept up. Breyman then proceeded about a mile, our men withdrawing before him. But when he reached the place where the road leaving the river flats ascends a hill...he was met by Warner with a body of fresh troops who captured some of his advanced parties and opposed his further advance with such spirit that he was eventually compelled to retire. He only reached the base of the hill alluded to—about a mile from the place where he first formed his men for fighting and where the firing first commenced.

Old Joshua Munro lived on the south side of the Wallomsac in sight of where Breyman first formed his men and saw the whole of their motions—their brass kettle drums glittering in the sun being a most striking feature of the scene.[53]

Heinrich Breymann

Lieutenant Colonel Heinrich Breymann provided this version of his defeat. In the controversy that ensued over who bore responsibility for the British disaster at Saratoga, Burgoyne hinted that both Breymann and Baum shared much of the blame because of their failure at Bennington. Neither officer was able to defend himself, however. Baum died on August 18 from wounds suffered at Bennington, while Breymann was killed at Bemis Heights on October 7.

On the 13th of August, at 8 o'Clock in the morning Sr. Francis Clarke, aid de Camp to his Excellency Genl. Bourgoyne brought me the order to march immediately with the Corps under my Command, consisting of a Bataillon of grenadiers, one of Chasseurs,[54] one Rifle Company & 2 pieces of Cannon to the Support of Lt. Colonel Baum.

I marched at 9 o'Clock and on Account of the Scarcity of Carts, I put two Boxes of Ammunition upon the Artillery Carts. Each Soldier Carried 40 Rounds in his Pouch.

The Troops being obliged to ford Battenscill, I was detained a considerable time by it. The number of hills, excessive bad Roads, and a continued Rain, impeded our march, so much, that we scarce made ½ English mile in an hour. Each gun & Ammunition Cart was obliged to be dragged up the Hills, one after an other. One Artillery Cart was overturned and with the greatest difficulty was put into a situation to proceed.

All these difficulties delayed us much, & notwithstanding every means was used and no trouble or labour spared, it was not possible for me to march faster. Our guide lost his way, & after a long search in vain, Major Barner was obliged to look for a Man who put us again in the right road.

All these Accidents prevented me from reaching Cambridge the evening of the 15th, & was therefore obliged to halt 7 miles this Side of it, where the men lay upon their Arms all night. Before I came to the place where I halted I wrote to Lt. Col. Baum to acquaint him with my coming to his support, Lieut. Hannemann went with this Account to Cambridge and from thence to Lt. Col. Baum's Post, where he arrived at 11 o'Clock at night; I received an answer the next morning. Early in the morning I marched on, but as the Artillery Horses had had no feed all the day before, and very little during the night, they were so weak as to be scarce able to drag the Cannon, on which Account our march was very slow.

Major Barner with the advanced Guard was obliged to go forwards to press horses, which we immediately made use of, and we continued our

BATTLE OF BENNINGTON
SECOND ENGAGEMENT
AUGUST 16ᵀᴴ 1777

AT THIS POINT OCCURRED THE DEFEAT OF COLONEL
BREYMAN WHO COMMANDED A FORCE OF 600 MEN SENT
BY GENERAL BURGOYNE TO REINFORCE COLONEL BAUM
COLONEL SETH WARNER AND HIS REGIMENT OF VERMONT
RANGERS "GREEN MOUNTAIN BOYS" DISTINGUISHED
THEMSELVES IN THIS ACTION.

ERECTED BY THE STATE OF NEW YORK
1927

Monument marking the second battle, the engagement with Breymann's command. *Author's collection.*

march as fast as possible, till about 2 miles, on other side of Cambridge, where I halted about ½ an hour to assemble the Troops.

About 2 o'Clock in the afternoon Colonel Skeene sent me two men, desiring an Officer and 20 Men to take possession of the Mill at Saint Coyk, which the Rebels intended possessing themselves of.

Instead of the Detachment which he asked for I sent a Captain Gleissenberg with the advanced Guard consisting of 60 Grenadiers & Chasseurs & 20 Riflemen.

I followed with the Column, as fast as possible. Upon this march an Ammunition Cart broke down. At ½ past 4 o'Clock in the afternoon, I reached the Mill, and found the advanced Guard in possession of it and all quiet.

I must positively declare, that neither during the march, nor even after I reached the Mill I did not hear a single shot fired, either from small arms or Cannon.

Colonel Skeene was at the Mill, and as he gave me to understand, that the Corps of Lt. Colonel Baum, was not above 2 Miles from me, I imagined I could not do better, than to push on to his Support. Colonel

Skeene was of the same Opinion, and we marched on over the Bridge, near the Mill endeavouring to reach Col. Baum, as soon as possible. At this time, I knew nothing of his engagement being over. If Col. Skeene knew it, I cannot conceive, what his reasons were, for concealing it from me. If I had known it I certainly should not have engaged the Enemy.

I had scarce passed the bridge 1000 yards, where, I perceived a considerable number of Armed People, some in jackets and some in Shirts, who were endeavouring to gain a height, which was on my left Flank.

I shewed these to Col. Skeene who assured me they were Regalists and rode up towards them and called out, but received no other Answer, than a discharge of fire Arm. I immediately ordered Major Barner's Bataillon to move off towards the heights; the Rifle Company and Grenadiers moved towards the right and than began the attack; and lasted till towards 8 o'Clock,

The Cannon were fired on the road where there was a blockhouse, which the Rebels left as soon as they began to fire upon it. Not withstanding fresh support was constantly coming into them, they were driven from every heights.

The Troops did their duty and every one concerned, did the same. As all the Ammunition was expended and the Cannon Ceased firing, nothing was more natural, than to expect the enemy would renew the Attack, which in fact was the Case.

I hastened with a Number of Men towards the Cannon, in order to bring them off. On this Occasion the Men received the most dangerous wounds, particularly Lt. Spangenberg, some Fire workers and some Artillery. The Horses were all killed, and if even one had been alive, it would not have been possible to have moved him.

I ordered them not to risque every thing and could not schorn the enemy's Fire, as soon as it was dark, I retired over the bridge, which I broke down, brought off as many of the wounded as I could and in Company with Col. Skeene arrived about 12 o'Clock at Cambridge, where, after taking the necessary precautions, I remained all night, and the next day the 17th I arrived at the Camp.

This is the best Account I can give of this whole Affair. The loss of my Cannon gives me the greatest concern. I did every thing in my power to save them, but the want of Ammunition prevented me, not only from returning the enemy's fire, but even of getting out of it, many lost their lives and limbs & could I have saved my Cannon, I would with pleasure have sacrificed my life to have affected it.
Signed,
Breymann, Lt. Colonel[55]

Other Accounts

Perley Howe

When he "turned out" to fight at Bennington, Perley Howe, a twenty-two-year-old Williamstown, Massachusetts resident, was on his sixth tour of duty since January 1776. Previously, he had served with both Seth Warner's regiment and local militia.

> *When the people of sd Williamstown heard that Col. Baum's force was marching into Vermont the Militia immediately turned out and he marched with them under Col. Simons and Captain Williams to Bennington at which place Capt. Jonathan Danforth took the Command of the Company by request of Capt. Williams who preferred serving under Danforth as the more experienced Man—on the third day after our arrival being the sixteenth day of August 1777 Col. Warner arrived with a reinforcement and Joined Gen. Stark and immediately attacked the British force. Col. Warner's reinforcement did not arrive until the commencement of the second engagement but Warner was there at the commencement of the Battle—Col. Simons Regiment in which P. Howe was serving was in both Battles and sd. Howe fought through the day.*[56]

Levi Beardsley

A member of the New York Senate, Levi Beardsley (1785–1857) was born near the Bennington battlefield eight years after the engagement. He preserved his family's stories of the action.

There had been occasional skirmishing before the final contest commenced; which was on the 16th of August, 1777. The previous day, an Indian chief had been shot by a party of militia men, concealed in a field of grain, as he with several of his warriors were riding along the road on horses that had been plundered from the inhabitants. A few days after the battle, an attempt was made to exhume his body, under an impression that possibly treasures might have been buried with him. When they came to the remains, one of the volunteers who had been engaged in the conflict, stood over the grave with an uplifted tomahawk, and exclaimed with stentorian voice, "arise, you old devil, arise." But the Indian gave no heed to the summons, nothing short of "the trump of the archangel" would ever wake that sleeper; and the treasure seeking whigs finding no inducement to further disturb the remains of the ghastly warrior.[57]

Solomon Safford

Solomon Safford's account helps show the "family" aspect of the battle. Three of his brothers—Samuel, who led the Green Mountain Boys regiment into the engagement, Joseph and Jacob, whose account appears earlier—fought at Bennington, as did his nephew, Samuel Safford Jr. Solomon, twenty-two, served as a private in the militia company commanded by Captain Samuel Robinson, his brother-in-law.

Solomon Safford of Bennington…says that at the time of Bennington Battle I resided in the family of Captn Saml Robinson, who commanded the west company of Militia of said town, the wife of said Robinson being my sister—that I turned out with said company & on the evening of the 15th of Augt was encamped with said company & the rest of Col. Brush's regt near the bend of the river about ½ a mile to the North of Genl Stark's encampment—that on the morning of the 16th Col. Brush with a part of the whole of his Regt including Capt. R's [Samuel Robinson's] company were ordered to Cross the river to the west of Genl Stark's encampment & attack the enemy's rear—By direction of Capt Robinson I remained with the knapsacks & other baggage during the day—I was well acquainted with Col. Warner whose family resided in town & on the morning of the battle Genl Stark & Col. Warner came past me on horseback & Genl Stark inquired what I was doing? I told him, & that I was there by order of my Captain. Col. Warner turned to Genl Stark & said, smiling at the

Seth Warner statue at the Bennington Battle Monument. *Author's collection.*

same time, *"the boy is doing right,"* to which Genl Stark assented & they passed on.

I cannot be mistaken in this, because I felt that Genl Stark's inquiry was an indirect imputation on my courage, & that Col. Warner who knew me had relieved me from any suspicion of that kind. I cannot say how long Col. Warner had been in Bennington at that time—I remember he was not in good health, & I have an impression he had been in Bennington some days.

I saw Warner's regiment pass toward the battle ground during the first action under the command of my brother Saml Safford. The heavy firing

in the first action lasted but a few minutes—the second action lasted two hours or more, & was much harder fighting & more lives lost in that than in the first.
Solomon Safford, October 1833[58]

Thomas Mellen

I enlisted at Francestown, New Hampshire, in Colonel Stickney's regiment, and Captain Clark's company, as soon as I learned that Stark would accept command of the State troops. Six or seven others from the same town joined the army at the same time. We marched forthwith to Number Four, and stayed there a week. Meantime I received a horn of powder, and run two or three hundred bullets. I had brought my own gun. Then my company was sent on to Manchester. Soon after I went with a hundred others under Colonel Emerson, down the valley of Otter Creek. On this excursion, we lived like lords on pigs and chickens in the houses of tories who had fled. When we returned to Manchester, bringing two hogsheads of West India rum, we heard that the Hessians were on their way to invade Vermont. Late in the afternoon of rainy Friday, we were ordered off for Bennington, in spite of rain, mud, and darkness. We pushed on all night, each making the best progress he could. About daybreak, I, with Lieutenant Miltimore, came near Bennington, and slept a little while on a hay-mow. When the barn-yard fowls waked us, we went for bread and milk to the sign of the Wolf, and then hurried three miles west to Stark's main body.

Stark and Warner rode up near the enemy to reconnoiter, were fired at with the cannon, and came galloping back. Stark rode with shoulders bent forward, and cried out to his men: "Those rascals know that I am an officer; don't you see they honor me with a big gun as a salute?" We were marched round and round a circular hill till we were tired. Stark said it was to amuse the Germans. All the while a cannonade was kept upon us from their breastwork. It hurt nobody, and it lessened our fear of the great guns. After a while I was sent with twelve others, to lie in ambush on a knoll a little north, and watch for tories on their way to join Baum. Presently we saw six coming towards us, who, mistaking us for tories, came too near us to escape. We disarmed them and sent them, under a guard of three, to Stark. While I sat on the hillock, I espied one Indian whom I thought I could kill, and more than once cocked my gun, but the orders were not to fire. He was cooking his dinner, and now and then shot at some of our people.

Between two and three o'clock the battle began. The Germans fired by platoons, and were soon hidden by smoke. Our men fired each on his own hook, aiming whenever they saw a flash. Few on our side had either bayonets or cartridges. At last I stole away from my post, and ran down to the battle. The first time I fired I put three balls into my gun. Before I had time to fire many rounds, our men rushed over the breastwork, but I and many others chased straggling Hessians in the woods.[59]

James Moor

A veteran of General Richard Montgomery's Canadian campaign, thirty-year-old James Moor fought in the New York militia. Baum's men seized his horse when they passed through Cambridge, New York, but he obtained revenge by serving with American forces on numerous scouting missions and skirmishes up to Burgoyne's surrender at Saratoga.

In the Summer of 1777 about the time Genl. Burgoyne brought the British forces to a place then called Skeensborough, now known by the name of White Hall, Deponent went to General Schuyler, who then lay at Fort Edwards, and engaged as a spy to watch the movements of the enemy. In this service he was engaged and watched the British forces so close that while they lay at Cambridge, he passed in the night through the whole camp. He remained in this service, and two days before the battle of Bennington himself, with some ten to twenty, were employed between the two Armies, as a scouting party and had several battles with parties of Indians that were engaged on the side of the British. And deponent feels confident that he killed two Indians, if not three, in these engagements. On the day of the battle of Bennington he joined the main Army and was engaged in that battle.[60]

William Post

William Post, thirty-two, reveals the varied duties that soldiers performed during the 1777 Northern Campaign, in addition to fighting at Bennington.

In the year 1777, Burgoyne came up the Lake to Tyconderoga and he went with Capt. & Lieu Smith with a large Scout to the frontiers to keep back the Enemy. he was about 13 miles North of Tyconderoga when given up and he was taken prisoner and carried to the flying Army called the Hessians commanded by Red Hazle. he was a prisoner Eight days when he escaped by stratagem and returned home. on his return at Manchester he told Capt. Warner what he had Seen while a prisoner and Col. Warner informed Genl. Stark and the General informed sd. applicant he must return the next morning with a Sufficient number of men to take what he had seen the Enemy bury under ground which was One Hogshead of Rum and two Barrells Shugar and other things which he took and returned to Manchester the same Night. The next day he went to Bennington where his family was then living and the next day was the 16th of August and he marched to the field of Battle called Bennington Battle.[61]

John Rowan

Born in Northern Ireland, New York militiaman John Rowan's account shows the importance of cattle and provisions, the same items that prompted Burgoyne to send Baum's command to Bennington. Rowan's statement also reveals the American attempts to suppress Loyalists.

Early in the Spring of the year 1777 he was called out in the Company of Militia aforesaid which he thinks was then commanded by Captain Armstrong in the Regiment commanded by Colonel Williams, and served in said company in and about the town of New Perth part of the time in building a Picket Fort in said town until on or about the 8th day of July when he was dismissed and the inhabitants in consequence of a communication Recd [received] by Colonel Joseph McCracken from General Schuyler were ordered…to move off and he [John Rowan] immediately took his family to St. Coicks. Having been engaged in actual service in said company as much as three months according to the best of this applicant's recollection and belief.

And within a week after he was dismissed in Captain Armstrong's company, he volunteered in the company of militia commanded by Captain Barnes in the Regiment commanded by Colonel Williams aforesaid. Recollects while in said company of going with Captain Barnes in a party of about twenty to seize some Cattle the enemy had placed in a field in New Perth. Also recollects that a short time before the Battle fought near Bennington he went in said company in a small party to take one Hicks [a Loyalist] of the enemy who was in the neighborhood by coincidence in New Perth, aforesaid, after cattle and provisions. Recollects that when Hicks was taken he was placed on the horse behind applicant and the horse was shot under them as they were returning to Mores in said town where Captain Barnes then lay.[62]

Benjamin Weed

A Lanesborough, Massachusetts resident, Benjamin Weed served as a recruiter in 1775 and was at Ticonderoga in both 1776 and 1777, before fighting at Bennington.

Shortly after we returned home as last mentioned, the alarm came that Col. Baum was coming with his German troops and we were ordered out to help defend the Country. I then belonged to Capt. Newell's Company, and was orderly sergeant of the same. I think it was on the 13th day of August in the said year 1777 that I left Lanesboro with said Company under the Command of Capt. Newell for Bennington. We arrived on the morning of the 16th of August at Bennington and joined Genl. Stark's troops who were then stationed there. And on the Same day we arrived the battle commonly called the battle of Bennington took place. And I with my company was engaged in it.

From out of my Company was killed Lieut. Nast, Lieut. Prindell, Waterman Eells, and Silas Ensign were killed.

At the request of my Captain I lent Silas ensign my horse, saddle, and bridle. Ensign was killed and I never got my horse, saddle, or bridle and I never received any compensation for them from the United States or any body else. The horse cost me £18 Massachusetts currency. After the battle of Bennington, I was detached with a part of men to guard a number of Tories, who were prisoners, and conduct them to Northampton, which I did and delivered them safe to the Gaol. There were 17 prisoners.[63]

Lemuel Stoddard

Serving in Colonel Thomas Stickney's regiment, Lemuel Stoddard, nineteen, reenlisted after fighting at Bennington, but like Alexander Magoon and many others, he contracted measles.

The first of August of the year that Burgoin was taken I went as one of the Milisa which Newhampshire were called upon to furnish. Kimball Calton was my Capt...I served at this time two months...I was in the Battle of Bennington, and was slightly wounded in my leg. Our forces were led into action by Genl. Stark. when in open view of the enemy, a Sergeant and four men were taken from our Company to go back in a certain direction and ascertain if the enemy had any force in reserve; I was one of the men; we were directed [to] creep along through a certain piece of woods on our hands and knees which we did. we soon discovered twelve of the enemy coming toward us. our Sergeant directed us to lie flat on the ground which we did and so remained until they came within about 2 rods. when we suddenly rose up our Sergeant ordered them to lay down their arms or they were dead men. The [sic] obeyed. he then ordered them to march back ten paces, they did so and we went and took up their arms, took them prisoners and returned to the main army, who were then engaged in action. a guard was put over the prisoners and we took our places in our Company and it was but a few minutes before I received a wound in my leg as before stated. I however continued through the Action. [64]

LOYALISTS

Peter Rosenbarica

A resident of Hoosic, New York, Peter Rosenbarica illustrates some of the experiences of Loyalists. Many, such as Peter and his brother, George, whose statement follows later, joined Burgoyne's army as it marched south toward Albany. Following the defeats at Bennington and then Saratoga, many of these Loyalists lost faith in the British cause and went into hiding in fear of American retaliation. Interestingly, both Rosenbaricas signed their memorials with an "X," indicating that they were illiterate. The similarity of the two statements suggests that the same person wrote or helped them compose the documents.

That Your Memorialist Joined his Majesties Army under the command of General Burgoyne at fort Edward on the 26th of July 1777—and Remained with said Army until they advanced to Fort Miller—when a Detachment was sent out from said army for Bennington & your

Memorialist made one of the Party & marched directly to St. Coick. Your Memorialist was left at St. Coick at Colo. John Van Rensellaers Mill with others to guard the mill and stores that was there—and Remained at said mill until after the Bennington Battle—then Hearing of the Defeat—and finding the army Retreating back Your Memorialist in Company with Capt. John Riter Immediately Repaired through the woods to Hosick aforesaid to his family—with an Intention if possible to take them into Camp at Saratoga, where the main army lay.

That Your Memorialist finding his family in such a Distressed Circumstance having all he had Pillaged away, & the American Scouts so thick that he Concluded it was Impossible to Return back without great Danger of falling into their hands and your Memorialist after Returning home as aforesaid, was obliged to Retire to his Loyal friends and Keep secreted, until the January following, when he applied to Major Banker who set him at Liberty, to be again seen in the Country without being taken up.[65]

George Rosenbarica

Like his brother, Peter, George Rosenbarica, a Hoosic resident, served with Baum's forces but went into hiding following the Battle of Bennington.

That your Memorialist Joined the British army under the Command of General Burgoyne—then at Fort Edward—and Remained with the Said army about three weeks—when a Detachment of Said army was sent out for to goe to Benington & he made one of the party.

That your Memorialist Took an active Part in the action at Benington—on the 16th of august 1777 and had his gun Shot to pieces in his hand—and when Said Party of the British Troops was Defeated and put to the Rout—he made his Escape and Returned home to Hosick aforesaid—and finding the american scouts to be so thick— he felt Timidated & Durst not venture to Return back to the main army—and Kept secreted in the woods and other secret places amongst his friends until the first of January 1778 when the Inclimancy of the Season obliged him to apply to Major Banker, who gave him Liberty to be openly seen and at Liberty.[66]

Samuel Anderson

Pownal, Vermont resident Captain Samuel Anderson served with the Loyalists whom Francis Pfister rallied to join Baum's command. Pfister's unit scattered following his death at Bennington. Some men returned home, while others, such as Anderson, escaped to Canada and continued to serve in other Loyalist units.

That your Memorialist was made Prisoner by the Rebels on or about the 15th day of May 1776 and Continued a Prisoner until the 28th day of July 1777 when he found means to make his escape out of the Goal at Litchfield in the State of Connecticut and made his way in the Night Season with much Difficulty through the woods to Pownal in the State of Vermont, it being about one hundred and ten miles; on your Memorialists arrival at Pownal aforesaid he immediately alarmed those people he had before Inlisted for the Kings Service, upon which they assembled to the Number of Sixty four men and forthwith proceeded with them & Joined the Detachmen of General Burgoynes Army sent against Bennington, and Fought there until they were obliged to Retreat, of the above mentioned Sixty four men, all but eight were killed and taken Prisoners by the Rebels in said action. Your Memorialist then Joined the Kings Army at Saratoga under the Command of General Burgoyne; and was there upon actual Service until the Convention took place, when he proceeded through the Woods to Ticonderoga.[67]

CATTLE AMBUSH ON THE HOOSIC RIVER

Although often forgotten, another battle was fought on August 16, the same day that Stark defeated Baum's and Breymann's commands. Fifty New Hampshire militiamen from Captains Stephen Parker's and Kimball Carleton's companies were returning to Bennington after having escorted cattle to General Horatio Gates's army near Stillwater, New York. That morning, somewhere near the junction of the Hoosic and Walloomsac Rivers, the soldiers crossed a bridge over a small stream. The men were hot and tired from their exertions, and many of them broke rank to get a drink and fill their canteens. As they did so, most of the column's advanced guard continued to march. Several moments later, a heavy volley erupted from a fence line to the left of the road. A group of Loyalists had spotted the

New Hampshire men and lay in ambush. If the soldiers had not stopped for water, the entire cattle escort could have been destroyed. As it was, the volley decimated the advanced guard. Parker's and Kimball's men quickly recovered and fought back. Lieutenant Samuel Cunningham, a French and Indian War veteran, then employed a shrewd ruse to trick the Loyalists into retreating. As the two sides traded fire, Cunningham loudly ordered another officer to attack the enemy's flank with five hundred additional men, who were not actually present. This supposed threat, coupled with the militiamen's fierce resistance, caused the Loyalists to break off the engagement, leaving behind some of their baggage. In this short, sharp action on the Hoosic River, four Americans were killed or mortally wounded, and five were wounded, three of whom never fully recovered. The Cattle Ambush on the Hoosic provides another aspect to the fighting near Bennington and the interactions between Whigs and Loyalists.

Abel Dutton

A seventeen-year-old who served in Captain Kimball Carleton's company, Abel Dutton later participated in the ill-fated 1779 Penobscot Expedition, one of the worst defeats in United States naval history.

> *A short time before Bennington battle he thinks in June 1777, he volunteered for three months under Capt. Carleton and Colo. Nichols regiment, marched to Charlestown N.H., staid there a few days and then marched to Manchester, Vt., staid there a short time, and then marched to Bennington, Vt. which place he marched about two days before the battle. Was in the advanced guard at the engagement, recollects laying down at a Spring to drink, when the guard were fired upon by a body of tories and several killed. Part of the guard with its Capt. retreated when the Lieut. assumed the command and the tories were driven back. After the battle marched with Genl Stark to Still Water, but on the way was attacked with the measles with which he was confined till his three months had expired.*[68]

Nehemiah Brown

Another seventeen-year-old who served in Kimball Carleton's company, Nehemiah Brown was from Westmoreland, New Hampshire. Seriously wounded in the cattle ambush, Brown sought to strengthen his application by including letters of support from Simian Cobb and William Hazeltine, who also fought in the skirmish.

> [I]*n the Spring of 1777 I was drafted to go against the British at Manchester in (now) Vermont, and in the vicinity of Bennington, in the militia service,…I continued in the service untill the day of the Battle of Bennington—on that morning I was coming into the battle from a service on which I with others, constituting a guard, had been detached on the day before, which service was to guard some cattle sent from Bennington to the north river—while on the march we were fired at by a party in ambush—three men were killed, John Raustad, Benoni Tisdale, Abel Gilbert. and I was wounded by a musket ball through my left leg at the calf, the ball passed between the bones of the leg as the surgeon stated and shattered the bones—I was then carried into Bennington on a horse, and was there ordered to return home, after having been there a few days, a horse was provided for me for that purpose, I returned to Westmoreland, and then came in a few days to Keene N.H. and placed myself under the care of Doct. Frink who had been appointed by the govt. to take care of wounded soldiers—I was there two or three months, and my leg did not entirely heal up under six months and has always from that time been troublesome to me…*

> *I was a soldier in Gen Stark's Brigade, I was in the vicinity of Bennington on the 16ᵗʰ of August 1777 when the battle of Bennington took place. I had been sent with a detachment, to guard a number of cattle from Bennington to Lanesburgh, on our return, we were attacked by a party of the enemy in or near Bennington, there were two soldiers with us by the name of Brown, both belonging to Westmoreland in the State of N. Hampshire and were both wounded; the name of one was Daniel, he was wounded through the arm and shoulder; the given name of the other I have forgotten, the wound was between the knee and ankle, and I think the bone not broken; I knew the last mentioned Brown perfectly well, and I do not now recollect when I last saw him, yet, am satisfied he now lives in Westmoreland as I very frequently hear from him, one of his Sons having resided in this town, and near to me for years past.*

When I joined the army in the year 1777 I resided in the aforesaid town of Westmoreland; we were detached to serve two months; I have no doubt the Brown last mentioned served out his time and more; including the time he must have been confined with his wound; at the time he received the ball in his leg myself and Ephraim Sawyer took him from the ground and carried him on our backs, until a horse was procured on which he was carried to Bennington, from whence he was sent to Westmoreland.
Simian Cobb, February 20, 1828

I was a soldier in Gen Stark's Brigade, and was in the vicinity of Bennington at the time of the battle there on the 16ᵗʰ of August. I was sent with a detachment to guard a number of cattle to Albany. Nehemiah Brown, of Westmoreland, went with me and was my messmate. On our return, we were attacked by a party of the enemy. The said Brown and I were in the same platoon. The said Brown was wounded in the leg and I was wounded in the arm, and am now on the pension list. When wounded, I went aside from the detachment and distinctly recollect that I saw the said Brown one or two days afterwards at Bennington suffering from the wound aforesaid.

Soon after he was wounded he obtained a parole and went to Keene N.H. where he remained some time under the care of a surgeon.

I further say that I served as a substitute for a man from Westmoreland—that our time of service was two months—and that the skirmish in which we were wounded was on the same day as the battle of Bennington.
William Hazeltine, January 30, 1828[69]

Amos Partridge

Amos Partridge saw extensive service in both the Massachusetts and New Hampshire militias prior to Bennington, fighting at Bunker Hill and doing a tour of duty at Fort Ticonderoga in 1777. He included statements in his pension application from the brothers of Simian Cobb, who wrote in support of Nehemiah Brown.

The Common Report was that Mr Amos Partridge went to Bennington in Vermont and was in that Battle. And Further more it was a Common Report that Amos Partridge was in the Skirmish with the British and toryes.

The Circumstance is as Follows. A Number Soldiers under Command of Lieutenant Hastings went to Stilwater with a Drove of Cattle and on their Return to Benington was Ambushed By A Large Number of British and toryes and a Number of Americans Killed and a Number wounded. Among the wounded was A man By Name of Brown and Belonged to putney in windham County in Vermont About 40 miles from Benington and was Sent home in this way. The Soldiers that went with him took from A Dutchman A Stallion horse to Convey him home on without Leave from the owner. The Dutchman made Application to general Starks then in Command for his horse. Knowing that the Applicant Being A Tory general Starks would Not give no Leave to have the horse given up.
Samuel Cobb, September 14, 1835

Mr. Partridge, I have Seen my Brother Simeon Cobb Since I Sent you My Brother Samuel's Affidavit. Brother Simeon Said that Brother Samuel was Correct Respecting the wounded man and the horse. He Said he himself was the man that took the Horse from the dutchman.
Nathaniel Cobb, October 11, 1835[70]

CIVILIANS

Levi Beardsley

Beardsley recorded the following accounts about Bennington, which provide additional insight into civilian interactions with both Indians and Germans. Obadiah Beardsley's house, indicated as F on the Durnford map, stood on the north side of the bridge over the Walloomsac. A German breastwork overlooked the cabin.

A considerable part of the contest was on my grandfather's farm, and in sight of his house; in fact the enemy commenced their breast work at his house; which being of logs was intended to be filled with men as a strong point of defence. Those who commenced building this breast work, were finally called away to man the works on the hills, and thus the house was left to the family…

My father was about fourteen years of age, and with a younger brother, was made prisoner by some lurking Indians, went in advance of the Hessians, and were part of the force sent on that expedition.

This hill, near the Walloomsac Bridge, contained a German breastwork, which initially held two cannons. The remains of this breastwork are still visible. The Obediah Beardsley cabin stood in the foreground, near the base of this hill. *Courtesy of Phyllis Chapman.*

The boys, when surprised and taken, were going to the pasture after cows; the Indians would not permit them to escape, though they treated them with kindness and whenever they attempted to turn out of the path, the Indians would press them in, by putting their guns by their side, telling them "not to strive." They were finally released by the interference of the Hessian officers, a short time before the battle, and with the rest of the family were shut up in the house. After the main force had been called away from the house, to man the works on the hill, a soldier came in and commenced pulling out the "chinking" between the logs, to enable him to fire out.

My grandfather remonstrated, and on the soldier persisting the old man seized his musket, and being a strong man wrenched it out of his hands and tossed it up into the chamber: then seizing him by the shoulders put him out by main force and fastened the door against him. The battle was sharply contested, but the result is known; the Hessians were defeated and taken, and a large body of them, when they surrendered, came running down the hill near the house with as little order as so many sheep, and surrendered in plain sight, several being shot, after they had ceased firing...

My father, who was very near the scene of action, and could hear every gun, used to compare the incessant reports with the constant snapping of hemlock brush when exposed to fire...

My grand-parents on my mother's side, resided in Cambridge, on the route that the enemy would take, and as they advanced, the country was filled with alarm and consternation. The cattle and live stock of all descriptions were driven off into Vermont, the iron ware and kitchen furniture buried and hid in the garden, while the wagon was placed before the door, where the horses were standing with their harness on, ready to start at a moment's warning. On the 13th or 14th of August, 1777, a man on horseback riding rapidly from the rear, came to warn the family to flee; telling them to be off at once, as the Indians were approaching, and were within a mile of the dwelling. Beds and bedding were hastily thrown into the wagon, and the family on top of them drove off towards Bennington.

As they went forward, they found the inhabitants flying like themselves; and soon after met a detachment of Americans under Col. Gregg, who had been sent forward by Gen. Stark, to the number of two hundred, to oppose and harass the Hessians and Indians. My mother, then about twelve years old, has often described the alarm that pervaded all classes.[71]

David and Elizabeth Gage

Ensign David Gage of Captain Jesse Wilson's company had seen extensive service prior to 1777. A Pelham, New Hampshire resident, he gave his company a bottle of West Indian rum in 1776, when he was appointed sergeant. The bottle remained in the family fifty-one years later. Gage's pension application shows the strong ties that soldiers maintain with their families while they are in service, something that remains true today. Elizabeth Gage's letter is in the same handwriting as Abel Gage, who attached a note to the bottom of it. This strongly suggests that Elizabeth was illiterate and asked a neighbor, in this case probably David's cousin, to write to her husband. Abel Gage served in Stark's regiment in 1776 and later applied for a pension.[72]

Bennington August 24ᵗʰ 1777

Loving Wife, these Lines Come With My Love to you Hoping they Will find you in good Helth threw the goodness of god as they Leave me. I have Had my Health Sinse I Left Home as Well as I Could Expect. I Have Not Heard anything from you Sense I Left Home. I Would inform you of ouer Victory over ouer Enemy as well Have Had Wonderful Success. ouer engagement Began about three of the Clock in the afternoon on Satterday the 16ᵗʰ instant and lasted the rest of That Day With a Little Sessation. I waus in the Bigest Part of it my self, But with the Blessing of god I waus Preserved and received nowt a wound and I myself may be able to give god the Praise for ouer victory. in all ouer army We Lost But 30 Killed and 40 Wounded and on the Enemy side a bout 300 Killed and 100 wounded and Seven Hundred taken Prisoners. As I Supose you Will Hear How it was Vary soon I Would inform you something ouer living which is vary good. Beaff and Bread in Plenty and Sars thats good. It is a genneral time of Helth in the army. in Left. Willsons Company theire was one Killed, one wounded that Waus John Kincaid Killed Josepth Rolings Wounded. Richard Barker Desiers to Be remembered to His Parents and sais that you tell them if you See them that He Has Had Something of an ill turn, But giting Better. I Have Nothing more to right only Pelham men are all in good Helth only the for mentioned ones.

I Would Have You Not fail to Right if an opportunity Will allow and if you Have an opportunity Subscribe it to Colo Moses Nichols Regemt, Left. Jesse Willsons Comapny.

So No more But I am your Loving Husband till Deth.
David Gage

Pelham August the 25 1777

Most Affectionate Husband after my kind Respects to you, hoping you are yet in the Land of the Living. I send you these lines to inform you that both I and the Child are in Good health at Present. Blessed be God for the Time and if ever these lines overtake you I hope they will find you under the Same Enjoyment. I have heard of the Battle that General Stark has had with the Enemy and I Expect that you and the rest of our Pelham men was in the Battle which makes me feel very Malancholy Expecting every Day to hear

Bad news from you But I hope for the Best for the Lord who is Able to Do all things can and will if he Sees fit Return you to your friends again. I would Inform you that it is a General time of health in this Place and they are all well at Father Atwood, and Desire to be Remembered to you. And your Brothers and Sisters are all well and Desire the same and Brother Pierece has Secured all your hay, into your Barn. Lieut. Willson's family are all well. I Should be Glad that you would Send us a letter as Soon as Possible. So no more at Present but I remain your Most affectionate Wife. Elizabeth Gage

Mr. Gage Sir,

As I have been writing I would Jest let you know that I am alive and that I long to be with you but I cannot. Remember me to all Pelham men. tell Amos Johnson that his family is well. any body that will take the trouble to Send me a line I shall receive it kindly and they shant be long without an answer from your friend
Abel Gage.

Bennington Sept. the 1ˢᵗ 1777

Loving Wife, I Have this time an opportunity to Right and Do gladly improve it to inform you that I am in the Land of the Living and in Perfect Helth and Bless Be god for it. And I Hope When these Lines Reach you they Will Find you in the Same state of Helth they Leave me. I Would inform you that I receiv'd your Letter With grait Pleasure to Hear that you waus in So Comfortable a State of Health and the Rest of my Friends. I Would inform you that I Have Ben in a Very Warm engagement in Which We Had Wonderfull Success as it is Likely you Have Heard more of the Perticulars than I Have time to Right. I Have Nothing Strange to Right only that Pelham men are all in Pritty good Health and order. Living is Vary good at Present for ouer money and that We have Plenty.

I Desire to Be remembered to Father Atwood and mother and all the Family and to my mother gage and my Brothers and Sisters and all inquiring Friends.

So No more But I am your Kind and Loving Husband
David Gage.[73]

Sarah Rudd

The wife of militia lieutenant Joseph Rudd, whose account appears earlier, Sarah Rudd's statement demonstrates the profound fear that many civilians felt as Burgoyne's army marched ever farther south.

> [I]t was an eventful year. I can never forget, while any thing of memory lives, my flight on horse-back, and in feeble health, with my babe and two other small children and my eldest daughter running on foot by the side of me from Bennington to Williamstown under circumstances of great alarm and fear from Hessians, tory-enemies, and Indians. and the absence of my husband at the time of this my trial for months before, and for months afterwards.
> Sarah Rudd[74]

Family fleeing danger. *Courtesy of the Granger Collection, New York, Item 0183453.*

Benjamin Weed

In the same year [1777] *I was again in the service as orderly sergeant in a company of Militia commanded by Capt. Ebenezer Newell of Lanesborough. We were ordered into the service about the middle of July, and marched from Lanesboro to Castleton in Vermont and there I was detached from the Company, with about thirty of my comrades for a guard to protect the women and children and assist them in flying from the British and Indians. And as near as I can recollect, Genl. Burgoyne was with his army at Fort Ann—having crossed Lake George. Our orders were to go to Fort Miller, but we were prevented from doing so by the Indians and Tories.*

Whilst on this detachment, at the fort of Pownall mountain, we counted the old men, women, and children with us, and they amounted to about 60. We escorted them to Williamstown and Lanesboro—where I remained till the alarm came to go to Bennington, as here after mentioned. I was on this last mentioned tour of service not less than one month and a half.[75]

Huldah Stewart

Huldah Stewart provided the following account of herself and her husband. John Stewart served as a volunteer at Bennington, where he captured a German soldier and kept his musket, sword and accoutrements as trophies, but his own house was plundered.

That early in July A.D. 1777, the said John Stewart resided with his family in Pawlet Vermont, then called the New Hampshire Grants, and that their neighborhood where they lived was alarmed by an express communicating the intelligence of the capture of Ticonderoga, and the disastrous result of the battle of Hubbardton and that the Indians attached to Burgoyne's army were ransacking the whole country. All the whigs who resided in that part of the country, were compelled to abandon their settlements at the north, and remove south to some place of greater security. That the said John Stewart having a team put forward his family, consisting of the applicant and three young children, and remained behind himself a few hours and endeavored to secrete some of his furniture, provisions, and other valuables, which were all however found, and stolen or destroyed by the tories, and with the exception of one iron Kettle, never recovered by the said Stewart. Among the rest, the leather bag before mentioned, containing the commissary and other papers relating to the military service of the said Stewart, was taken, and all the papers destroyed, fragments of them having been found strewed upon the ground for a considerable distance from the house.

After suffering great hardship, the applicant with her children was placed in the family of her father in Bennington, where she remained until Nov. after the surrender of Burgoyne.[76]

Hannah Wheeler

Hannah Wheeler was ninety-two when she unsuccessfully applied for a pension in her husband's name. David Wheeler of Lanesborough, Massachusetts, commanded a company in Colonel Benjamin Simonds's militia regiment.

[He] *was gone from home so much on alarms, that I wanted to have him resign, and he did, and was discharged, but the Company immediately chose him again, and he served till the war was over: One time when I had a child thirteen days old Colonel Simons Sent to him* [a message] *that*

Minutemen of the Revolution. *Courtesy of the Library of Congress, cph.3a52571, http://www.loc. gov/pictures/resource/cph.3a52571.*

he must go to Ticonderoga, this was in December and he went and was gone all winter and I think did not return till April: When Independence was Declard, he was at Fort Anne: He went to the Bennington Battle and four men in his Company were killed, two of them had families; it was rumoured that he was killed and when he returned I cryed, and he asked me if I was sorry but I told him I was crying for joy—He brought home some Hessian Officers to our house, and I declined shaking hands with them, but got them victuals. He was in the battle at Fort Anne: He went out on all the alarms, and Colonel Simons who lived in Williamstown was his Colonel and Sent Down orders for him to go—he was called out a great many times in a year: One time every blanket in the house was taken by his soldiers, and always all provisions and blankets that his men wanted.[77]

Lucy Meacham

Lucy Meacham's husband, Isaac, was born on Christmas Day 1748. The Williamstown, Massachusetts resident served in the Lexington Alarm and fought at Bunker Hill in 1775. He left his wife and one-week-old son to fight at Bennington, something that she recounted many years later.

That said Isaac Meacham, this applicant's Husband was a volunteer at the Bennington Battle which was fought on the 16th day of August AD 1777. This applicant recollects this from the fact that her first born son, John Meacham, was then but one week old, who was born August 7, 1777 and during her husband's absence at that Battle, Timothy Brewster, who now resides in Ellisburgh, Jefferson County, and State of New York remained with her, and her said husband was about at this particular time in the service of his country as a Soldier six or eight days, and in which time he was actually engaged in the battle of Bennington under Col. Starke.
Lucy Meacham

That deponent staid at the house of Isaac Meacham when he was absent at the Bennington Battle. The Reverant Timothy Brewster…was at said Isaac Meacham's house while he was absent at that Battle. That deponent's Sister said Lucy Meacham was then confined with her first born Son John Meacham. That her husband said Isaac Meacham was absent

at the time the Bennington Battle was fought about a week and deponent was in no doubt but said Isaac Meacham was actually engaged in said Battle under Colonel Starks.
Lydia Meacham

That in the year of our Lord 1777, he was personally acquainted with Isaac Meacham and Lucy Meacham his wife. That he was in Williamstown... at the time of the Battle of Bennington on the 16ᵗʰ of August A.D. 1777. That when the country was alarmed by the progress of the British troops towards Bennington my oldest brother Daniel Brewster (living then about a mile from said Isaac Meacham) and that said Isaac Meacham, and other militia turned out and went up as soldiers towards Bennington and after being absent some days they returned and this deponent staid one night at said Isaac Meacham's house while he was absent. His wife being then confined to bed with her first child John Meacham who was then about one Week old.
Timothy Brewster [age eighteen in 1777][78]

Syverius Rice

Syverius Rice was seventy-three and residing in Michigan when he provided a supporting statement for his sister, Rachel Perry, who was the widow of a Bennington veteran, Winslow Perry.

That he resided with his Father's family in the State of Vermont in the time of the war of the Revolution. That he well remembers the time that his Sister Rachel Rice was married to Winslow Perry from these facts. That her Mother was opposed to the Match and when Mr. Perry asked consent I was present. He did not come himself but Sent another man and after a great deal of conversation She (meaning the mother of said Rachel) said they might do as they pleased and of his sister Rachel being a favorite and at the time she was going off to get married to said Winslow Perry this deponent cried and took hold of his sister Rachel's clothes and asked why Mr. Perry could not take one of the other girls instead of Rachel. And this deponent can well remember the Battle of Bennington that his father came into the house and said that the enemy was upon them and they must flee and they packed up and went over the mountains from Shaftsbury and he was carried on horseback.[79]

AFTERMATH

JOSEPH RUDD

In the days following the battle, soldiers on both sides and civilians had to adjust to new circumstances and resume their lives. In the following letter, Joseph Rudd, who appeared earlier in this book, informed his father of the events of the battle, including his wife Sarah's flight. Rudd's letter also shows how personal the engagement was, as neighbor fought neighbor, including Loyalist Samuel Anderson, whose statement appeared earlier.[80]

Bennington, Aug. the 20th, 1777

Honored Father:—After my duty I take this opportunity to write to you, hoping these few lines will find you well, as through the goodness of God they leave me and my family. We met with a great deal of trouble on the 16th instant. Myself and brother John was preserved through a very hot battle. We killed and took according to the best account we can get, about one thousand of the enemy. Our loss was about thirty or forty. We marched right against their breastworks with our small arms, where they fired upon us every half minute, yet they never touched a man. We drove them out of their breastworks and took their field pieces and pursued and killed great numbers of them. We took four or five of our neighbors—two Sniders and two Hornbecks. The bigger part of Dutch Hoosick was in the battle against us. They went to the Reglers a day or two before the fight. Samuel Anderson, was a captain amongst the Reglers, and was in the battle against

us. Whilst I was gone my wife and children went off and got down to Williamstown. After I got home I went after them and found them to Landlord Simons.* I have got them home again. My wife was very much tired out. She had four children with her. Belindy [Celinda] was forced to run on foot. We soon expect the enemy will come upon us again and what shall I do with my family I know not.
JOSEPH RUDD.
Col. Simonds.[81]

JOHN BURGOYNE'S ASSESSMENT

On August 26, Burgoyne announced to his army the findings of his investigation into the defeat at Bennington. He complimented the soldiers and their officers for their bravery and duty and blamed most of the results on bad luck and "common Accidents of War." He did find fault with "those who managed the Department of intelligence," a reference to Philip Skene, who had accompanied Baum. Skene was an obvious target because he shared some of the responsibility for the defeat, and he held no official rank.

August 26, 1777:

The Lieut. General having received the report from Lt. Col. Breymann, relative to the affair at Saintwick Mills, and also having obtained every collateral information possible, thinks it justice to declare publickly, that he has no reason to be dissatisfied with the personal Spirit of the Officers and Troops in the Action; that on the contrary the Officers who commanded the different Corps acted with intrepidity.

The failure of the Enterprize seems in the first Instance to have been owing to the Credulity of those who managed the Department of intelligence, suffered great numbers of the Rebel Soldiers to pass and repass, and perhaps count the numbers of the Detachment, and upon ill-founded confidence induced Lieut. Col. Baume to advance too far to have a secure retreat. The next cause was the slow movement of Lieut. Col. Breymann's Corps, which from bad weather, bad Roads, tired horses and other impediments stated by Lieut. Colo Breymann, could not reach 24 miles from eight in the morning of the 15th to four in the afternoon of the 16th. The Succour therefore arrived too late. The failure of Ammunition, in the management of which there appears to have been improvidence, was another misfortune. The rest seem common Accidents of War. Upon the whole the Enemy have severely felt their little success, and there is no circumstance to affect the Army with further regret or melancholy, than that which arises from the loss of some gallant men. But let the Affair of the Mill at Saintwick remain henceforward as a lesson against the impositions of a treacherous Enemy, many of whom in the very hour of swearing allegiance to the King, fought against his Troops, and against expending Ammunition too fast, by which conquering Troops were obliged to retire with loss. The Reflection upon this Affair will moreover excite Alertness and Exertion in every Corps marching for the support of another, by shewing in whatever degree those qualities may be possessed by the Commanding Officer (and they are not doubted in the present instance), yet unless they are general, common accidents may become fatal, and the loss of two hours may decide the turn of an enterprise, and it might happen in some cases, the fate of a Campaign.[82]

JOHN BURGOYNE TO LORD GEORGE GERMAIN, AUGUST 20, 1777 (PRIVATE)

While Burgoyne publicly dismissed Bennington's significance, his private appraisal was much grimmer. In this letter to the British war minister, Burgoyne attempted to justify his reasons for embarking on the expedition and why it failed. He clearly blamed both Baum and Breymann but would not do so openly. The defeat also made Burgoyne doubt the Loyalists, both their numbers and their attachment to the British cause.

In regard to the affair at Saintcoick, I have only to add to the public account, that if ever there was a situation to justify enterprise and exertion, out of the beaten track of military service, it was that in which I found myself. Had I succeeded, I should have effected a junction with St. Leger, and been now before Albany. And I flatter myself, I need only mention those views, to shew that in hazarding this expedition I had the soundest principles of military reasoning on my side, viz. that the advantages to be expected from success were in a great degree superior to the evils that could attend miscarriage. The secondary purposes, to which I alluded in the public letter, were to try the affections of the country; to complete the Provincial corps, many recruits for which were unable to escape from their villages without a force to encourage and protect them; and to distract the councils of the enemy, by continuing their jealousy towards New England.

Major General Reidesel has pressed upon me repeatedly the mounting [of] his dragoons, the men were animated with the same desire, and I conceived it a most favourable occasion to give into their ideas and solicitations, because in exerting their zeal to fulfill their favourite purpose, they necessarily would effect the greater purpose of my own. The rest of the troops were selected from such as would least weaken the solid strength of the army, in case of ill success; and I thought it expedient to take a little trial of the Provincials and Canadians before I might have occasion for them in more important actions.

The original detachment could not have been made larger without opening roads, and other preparations of time, nor should I have thought it justifiable to expose the best troops to loss upon a collateral action. Had my instructions been followed, or could Mr. Breymann have marked at the rate of two miles an hour any given twelve hours out of the two and thirty, success would probably have ensued, misfortune would certainly have been avoided. I did not think it prudent, in the present crisis, to mark these circumstances to the public so strongly as I do in confidence to your Lordship, but I rely, and I will venture to say I expect, because I think justice will warrant the expedition, that while, for the sake of public harmony, that necessary principle for conducting nice and laborious service, I colour the faults of the execution, your Lordship will, in your goodness, be my advocate to the King, and to the world, in vindication of the plan.

The consequences of this affair, my Lord, have little effect upon the strength or spirits of the army; but the prospect of the campaign in other respects, is far less prosperous than when I wrote last. In spite of St. Leger's victory, Fort Stanwix holds out obstinately. I am afraid the expectations of Sir J. Johnson greatly fail in the rising of the country. On this side I find daily reason to doubt the sincerity of the resolution of the professing loyalists. I have about 400, but not half of them armed, who may be depended upon; the rest are trimmers, merely actuated by interest. The great bulk of the country is undoubtedly with the Congress, in principle and in zeal; and their measures are executed with a secrecy and dispatch that are not to be equaled. Wherever the King's forces point, militia, to the amount of three or four thousand assemble in twenty-four hours; they bring with them their subsistence, & c. c. and, the alarm over, they return to their farms. The Hampshire Grants in particular, a country unpeopled and almost unknown in the last war, now abounds in the most active and most rebellious race of the continent, and hangs like a gathering storm upon my left… [83]

COMMEMORATION

M any veterans remembered Bennington as an important event in their lives, and several referred to the battle as "memorable." Some returned to the battlefield, just as former soldiers have done for centuries and continue to do today. Captain Peter Kimball, who received a slight wound there, "went to see the ground where the battle was" three times in the two weeks following the action. He made his final visit on Saturday, August 30, accompanying a newly arrived company from his hometown, Boscawen, New Hampshire. Kimball seemingly wanted to share with his neighbors the site where he and his fellow soldiers faced the full gamut of human emotions to win a decisive victory against a fearsome opponent. Similarly, Thomas Abell, a sergeant in the Bennington militia, remembered his participation and demonstrated its importance by taking his son to the battlefield. Abell wanted the young boy to understand what he had done there.[84]

Veterans were not the only people to visit the battle site and recognize its importance. One man reported seeing "hundreds of visitors…from all the surrounding country" on the field three days after the engagement, while Thomas Jefferson and James Madison toured it in 1791. Over time, some people continued to regard the battleground as a sacred site, but visits declined, as did knowledge of the field. In the fall of 1830, a number of travelers made a "pilgrimage" to Bennington "to visit a spot hallowed in American history—to tread that field, sacred to liberty, where the cause of the Colonies first began to brighten." When they traveled several miles west

The Bennington Battle Monument with the John Stark statue. *Courtesy of Phyllis Chapman.*

to the actual battlefield, however, they found that local residents frequently knew little or nothing about it. "On being asked to point out the battlefield, they were unable to do it, and expressed some surprise at so apparently uncommon a question."[85]

If knowledge of the actual battleground had diminished by the 1830s, this was not true of the battle itself. Nearly every Bennington veteran had fought alongside his brothers, neighbors and friends on that fateful day on the Walloomsac. If these men had failed to do their duty, they would have betrayed not only the American cause but also their own families. Under such circumstances, there was little doubt that the people back home would have soon learned of this. But this did not happen. Instead, they heard stories about the veterans' heroic deeds on "Hessian Hill" and at the "Tory Redoubt," and these became familiar tales in numerous towns and villages throughout New York and New England. Many years later, Bennington veterans frequently included supporting statements from neighbors when they applied for pensions. These accounts usually noted that the former soldier was widely known for having fought at the battle.

In 1849, fifteen residents from Newark and Arcadia, New York, signed a petition requesting a pension for Samuel Dewey, who, at age fourteen, served as a teamster transporting wounded soldiers from the field. A neighbor noted that Dewey was memorable because he knew the battleground well, often referred to old Bennington inhabitants and used the river's archaic name, Walloomschoick. The same could be said for Samuel Sutton, a private in Captain Benjamin Sias's New Hampshire Company, who reportedly "was one of the first who leaped over the breastwork of the enemy." An acquaintance wrote that to doubt that Sutton fought at Bennington was as "absurd" as to "deny that Franklin Pierce occupies the White House at this time."[86]

One factor that helped keep the battle's memory alive was that veterans and their neighbors participated in commemorative ceremonies marking its anniversary. These events, held sporadically during the war but becoming more organized in the 1780s and beyond, usually took place in Bennington itself, not on the battlefield. The ceremonies featured music, orations and fireworks and often had different emphases, such as promoting Vermont statehood or anti-British sentiments in the years before 1812. Still, remembering the veterans' crucial role always remained prominent. In 1790, the *Vermont Gazette* wrote, "May the recollection of the tranquil effects of the martial deeds, achieved by our venerable fathers and heroes, on this important and auspicious day, fill every heart with honorable transport."[87]

"Six Aged Citizens of Bennington." This daguerreotype, taken in September 1848, shows six men who were children or young adults at the time of the battle. Samuel Safford Jr., seated on the right end, fought at Bennington, as did his father and three uncles. At age sixteen, he was reputedly the first American to storm the dragoon breastwork. *Courtesy of the Bennington Museum, Bennington, VT, Image A901.*

The ceremonies also featured veterans as participants, regardless of from what state they hailed. Captain Daniel Brown, of the Massachusetts militia, "for many years went to Bennington to celebrate the anniversary of the said Battle."[88] The same was true for Vermonter Joseph Rudd, who grappled with a German soldier in the breastwork and whose wife fled to Massachusetts with Baum's approach. A neighbor recalled that Rudd always participated in these events and held a "place of honor among the band of surviving heroes and veterans who fought for Independence."

Not surprisingly, these events also kept John Stark's memory alive. On August 16, 1806, the "numerous and respectable body of Republican citizens" attending the ceremony sent Stark its highest regards. "The few officers and soldiers yet living, who were immediately under your command, still hail you as their fortunate and brave general; while those who were their children or unborn, hail you as the patriot of your country." Three years later, over sixty Bennington veterans were among those who attended a meeting to plan that year's event, and they decided to invite Stark. "No event could so animate the brave 'sons of liberty,' as to see their venerable leader and preserver once more in Bennington: that their young men may once have the pleasure of seeing the man who so gallantly fought to defend their sacred rights, their fathers and mothers." Realizing that he might be unable to attend, they requested that Stark at least send a message to the audience.[89]

The general, age eighty-one, reluctantly declined the invitation, but he did send a letter, as the organization committee requested. Addressed to "My Friends and Fellow-Soldiers," the letter was widely republished by newspapers. Referring to his "men that had not learned the art of submission, nor had they been trained to the art of war," Stark reiterated his belief in the United States. More importantly, he urged his listeners to remain vigilant, just as his soldiers had thirty-two years earlier. Stark then closed his letter with a famous postscript that undoubtedly resonated with the Bennington veterans and their families and continues to inspire Americans to this day: "Live free or die—Death is not the greatest of evils."

O.C. Merrill

A longtime friend of the family, O.C. Merrill submitted a statement in 1837 on behalf of Sarah Rudd when she applied for a pension in her husband Joseph Rudd's name.

> *I have known the family of Lt. Rudd deceased for about 40 years. I knew Lt. Rudd until his death and I was present at his funeral. In his life time I have heard him speak of his services, perils and trials during the revolutionary war. of his personal encounter with a Hessian in the battle of Bennington, and have seen the sword he took from him, and brought home, and kept as a trophy. I have heard others relate it. He was always spoken of by the late Col. Samuel Robinson, and others as one who had done much service, and as a brave officer. In all our commemorative occasions, which until late years, were annually observed, he was always in the arrangement of the day put in the place of honor among the band of surviving heroes and veterans who fought for Independence.*[90]

APPENDIX A

JOHN STARK

My Friends and Fellow-Soldiers,

I received your's of the 22d inst. Containing your fervent expression of friendship, and your very polite invitation to meet with you, to celebrate the 16ᵗʰ of August in Bennington. As you observe, I "can never forget, that" I "commanded American troops" on that day in Bennington. They were men that had not learned the art of submission, nor had they been trained to the art of war. But our "astonishing success" taught the enemies of liberty, that undisciplined freemen are superior to veteran slaves—And I fear we shall have to teach the lesson anew to that perfidious nation.

Nothing could afford me more pleasure than to meet "the sons of liberty" on that fortunate spot. But, as you justly appreciate, the infirmities of old age will not permit, for I am now four score and one years old, and the lamp of life is almost spent. I have, of late, had many such invitations, but was not ready, for there was not oil enough in the lamp.

Statue of John Stark at the Bennington Battle Monument. *Courtesy of Phyllis Chapman.*

You say you wish your young men to see me, but you who have seen me can tell them, that I never was worth much for a show, and certainly cannot be worth their seeing now.

In case of my not being able to attend, you wish my sentiments; them you shall have, as free as the air we breathe. As I was then, I am now—The friend of the equal rights of men, of representative democracy, of republicanism, and the declaration of independence, the great charter of our national rights: and of course the friend of the indissoluble union and constitution of the states. I am the enemy of all foreign influence, for all foreign influence is the influence of tyranny. This is the only chosen spot of liberty—this is the only republic on earth...

It is my orders now, and will be my last orders to my volunteers, to look well to their sentries...

I shall remember gentlemen, the respect you, and "the inhabitants of Bennington, and its neighbourhood," have shewn me, till I go to the country from which no traveler returns. I must soon receive marching orders.

John Stark.

P.S. I will give you my volunteer toast—Live free or die—Death is not the greatest of evils.[91]

Appendix B

BENNINGTON EXPEDITION TIMELINE

May 8, 1777	Burgoyne arrives in Quebec from England with plans for the forthcoming campaign.
June 20	The main body of Burgoyne's army begins to assemble at Cumberland Head on Lake Champlain.
June 21	Burgoyne arrives at the Bouquet River and meets with the Indians, who accompany his army.
June 22	Burgoyne issues a proclamation calling on civilians to support the Crown's efforts and promising retribution to those who resist.
June 28	The main body of the British army arrives at Crown Point.
July 1	Burgoyne's army lands several miles from Fort Ticonderoga and begins to encircle it over the next several days.

July 4 British troops occupy Mount Defiance, also called Sugarloaf Hill, overlooking the fort and making it untenable.

July 5 The Americans evacuate Fort Ticonderoga. Part of the army retreats southeast into Vermont, while the rest travels by water down South Bay to Skenesborough.

July 6 Pursuing British warships overtake the Americans near Skenesborough, capturing large quantities of military supplies. Burgoyne establishes his headquarters there.

July 7 British and German troops scatter the American rear guard led by Colonel Seth Warner at Hubbardton, Vermont, after a sharp fight. Warner withdraws to Manchester.

July 10 Burgoyne sends Riedesel and most of his command to Castleton, Vermont, to procure supplies and raise Loyalists.

July 15 The Vermont Committee of Safety calls on neighboring states for aid.

July 18 Meeting in a special session, the New Hampshire General Court votes to raise a three-regiment brigade commanded by John Stark to resist the British invasion.

July 22 Riedesel proposes an expedition into the Hampshire Grants to gather horses and cattle to mount the German dragoons and ease the army's transportation problems.

Bennington Expedition Timeline

July 24   Stark arrives at Fort Number 4, Charlestown, New Hampshire, and begins organizing his command as troops arrive.

July 25   The British army advances from Skenesborough to Fort Anne. Riedesel's Germans march from Castleton to Skenesborough.

July 29   Burgoyne's army arrives at Fort Edward on the Hudson River.

August 4   Burgoyne decides to send an expedition into the Hampshire Grants but greatly modifies Riedesel's initial proposal.

August 6   Stark marches for Manchester with three hundred soldiers, having already forwarded seven hundred.

August 7   Stark arrives at Manchester and meets with Warner and Benjamin Lincoln.

August 8   Stark arrives at Bennington.

August 9   Baum and part of Burgoyne's army advance to Fort Miller.

August 11   Baum begins his expedition, but Burgoyne redirects him to Bennington.

August 13   Baum marches to Cambridge, New York. Learning that Indians were near this village, Stark sends Lieutenant Colonel William Gregg to Sancoick with two hundred men.

August 14	Baum arrives at Sancoick, skirmishes with Gregg and pursues when he retreats. Stark marches to Gregg's aid and meets Baum near Walloomscoick, New York, five miles west of Bennington.
	Baum entrenches and sends a message to Burgoyne requesting reinforcements. Loyalists, including Francis Pfister, join Baum's command and continue to do so until the battle.
	Stark summons the Green Mountain Boys regiment and local militia for help.
August 15	Heavy rain prevents a general engagement, but Stark probes Baum's defenses and plans an attack. Additional American militiamen arrive at Stark's camp.
August 16	Morning: Loyalists ambush an American cattle escort returning from the Hudson River. Stark sends Nichols and Herrick to encircle Baum's left and right flanks, respectively.
3:00 p.m.	Nichols opens the American attack on the dragoon fortification atop the hill and is joined by Herrick. Meanwhile, Stark's other troops storm the "Tory Redoubt" and Baum's position near the bridge. The Americans kill or capture nearly all of Baum's command.
4:30 p.m.	Breymann comes under fire just beyond the Sancoick Bridge, deploys his troops and begins to drive back Stark's scattered forces. The Green Mountain Boys and fresh Massachusetts militia stiffen the American line and defeat Breymann, who retreats in the darkness.
August 18	Baum and Pfister die of their wounds.

Bennington Expedition Timeline

September 13	Burgoyne crosses the Hudson River, resuming his advance on Albany after a nearly month-long delay caused by Bennington.
September 19	The Americans defeat Burgoyne at the Battle of Freeman's Farm.
October 7	The Americans defeat Burgoyne at the Battle of Bemis Heights. Breymann is killed in the fighting.
October 17	Burgoyne surrenders at Saratoga.
February 6, 1778	France and the United States sign a military alliance.

Appendix C

KEY PERSONALITIES APPEARING

IN THE ACCOUNTS

FRIEDRICH S. BAUM (circa 1727–1777) possessed extensive military experience in Europe, but he could not speak English. Still, Burgoyne selected him to lead the Bennington expedition, as the commander of the Dragoon Regiment Prinz Ludwig. He was mortally wounded during the engagement and died on August 18.

HEINRICH BREYMANN (1727–1777), the third ranking German officer in Burgoyne's army, commanded the column sent to Baum's aid. His slow rate of march, coupled with rumors of a personal dispute with Baum, led some to suggest that Breymann purposely took his time. Reputedly a strict disciplinarian, he was killed on October 7 at the Battle of Bemis Heights, possibly by one of his own men, as the Americans overran his position.

JOHN BURGOYNE (1722–1792) had served in America since 1775, after having achieved a solid record during the Seven Years' War. A playwright and member of Parliament, Burgoyne is best remembered for the ill-fated Saratoga Campaign and the subsequent controversy over who bore responsibility for the disaster.

WILLIAM GREGG (1730–1824) had commanded a minuteman company that marched to Boston in the spring of 1775 and served in the 1776 New York Campaign. He was the lieutenant colonel in Moses Nichols's regiment of Stark's brigade at Bennington. Gregg's skirmish with Baum at the Sancoick Bridge on August 14 helped set the stage for the main battle two days later.

SAMUEL HERRICK (1732–1798) commanded the Vermont Regiment of Rangers. Stark dispatched him to the left with a large detachment of mainly Vermont troops to encircle Baum's rear.

DAVID HOBART (1722–1799), the colonel of the Twelfth New Hampshire Militia Regiment prior to the Bennington Campaign, commanded Stark's smallest regiment. He was one of the two colonels who led the attack on the Loyalist breastwork south of the Walloomsac River.

MOSES NICHOLS (1740–1790), a physician by training, commanded one of Stark's regiments at Bennington. He led the column that attacked Baum's right rear.

FRANCIS PFISTER (circa 1740–1777) was a German-born military engineer who served in the Sixtieth Regiment of Foot, the Royal Americans, during the French and Indian War. Settling near Hoosic, New York, in 1774, he raised a Loyalist force that joined Baum's command. Like Baum, Pfister received a mortal wound at Bennington and died two days later.

JOHN RAND (1722–1789) commanded the Worcester County, Massachusetts militia companies from Colonel Job Cushing's regiment. Their arrival, late in the battle, helped turn the tide against Breymann.

FRIEDERICH ADOLPHUS RIEDESEL (1738–1800) headed the German auxiliary troops with Burgoyne. He opposed Baum's expedition to Bennington.

SAMUEL ROBINSON (1738–1813) commanded one of the two companies of Bennington militia that fought at the battle.

SAMUEL SAFFORD (1737–1813) served as the lieutenant colonel in Seth Warner's Green Mountain Boys regiment. He commanded the regiment as it marched from Manchester to Bennington because Warner had already joined Stark.

BENJAMIN SIMONDS (1726–1807) commanded a regiment of Berkshire County, Massachusetts militia at the battle. Some sources suggest that he was not personally on the field.

Key Personalities Appearing in the Accounts

PHILIP SKENE (1725–1810) was a former British army officer who attempted to establish an estate on the southern end of Lake Champlain following the French and Indian War. Skene is sometimes blamed for convincing Burgoyne to march overland to Fort Edward from Lake Champlain, a move that cost the British general three weeks. He accompanied Baum on the Bennington expedition and bore some responsibility for the defeat.

JOHN STARK (1728–1822), the American commander at Bennington, had seen extensive service both in the French and Indian War and in the early stages of the Revolution. He decimated the British light infantry at Bunker Hill and spearheaded the attack at Trenton before resigning his commission in a dispute over promotion. He is best remembered for writing, "Live free or die—Death is not the greatest of evils," New Hampshire's state motto.

THOMAS STICKNEY (1729–1809) held multiple military and local civil offices in New Hampshire. He commanded one of Stark's three militia regiments at Bennington, where he fought at the "Tory Redoubt."

SETH WARNER (1743–1784), one of the original leaders of the Green Mountain Boys along with Ethan Allen, participated in the taking of Fort Ticonderoga on May 10, 1775, and seized Crown Point two days later. Elected colonel of the regiment when it entered Continental service, Warner fought in Richard Montgomery's Canadian Campaign. The British roughly handled the Green Mountain Boys at Hubbardton, but Warner gained revenge at Bennington, where he played a key role in assisting Stark.

NOTES

PREFACE

1. For information on pensions for Revolutionary War veterans, see John Resch, *Suffering Soldiers: Revolutionary War Veterans, Moral Sentiment, and Political Culture in the Early Republic* (Amherst: University of Massachusetts Press, 1999). Also see Maureen Taylor, *The Last Muster: Images of the Revolutionary War Generation* (Kent, OH: Kent State University Press, 2010), especially 124–25, for an interesting study that features photographs of Revolutionary War veterans, including some from the Battle of Bennington.

2. All quotes are found in the documents in this book unless otherwise noted, such as these two: John Burgoyne, *A State of the Expedition from Canada, as Laid before the House of Commons, by Lieutenant-General Burgoyne, and Verified by Evidence; with a Collection of Authentic Documents, and an Addition of Many Circumstances Which were Prevented from Appearing before the House by the Prorogation of Parliament* (London: J. Almon, 1780), 93; Thomas Jefferson to John Stark, August 19, 1805, Thomas Jefferson Papers, American Memory, Library of Congress, http://memory.loc.gov/ammem/collections/jefferson_papers/index.html (accessed April 13, 2011).

3. One exception is Peter Aichinger, trans., ed., *At War with the Americans: The Journal of Claude-Nicolas-Guillaume de Lorimier* (Victoria, BC: Press Porcepic, 1981). De Lorimier served with the Indians at Bennington, where he received a leg wound.

THE BENNINGTON EXPEDITION

4. Michael P. Gabriel, *Major General Richard Montgomery: The Making of an American Hero* (Madison, NJ: Fairleigh Dickinson University Press, 2002); Douglas R. Cubbison, *The American Northern Theater Army in 1776: The Ruin and Reconstruction of the Continental Force* (N.p.: McFarland & Company, Inc., Publishers, 2010). For the origins and details of the Saratoga Campaign, see Richard M. Ketchum, *Saratoga: Turning Point of America's Revolutionary War* (New York: Henry Holt, 1997); Hoffman Nickerson, *The Turning Point of the Revolution, Or Burgoyne in America* (1928; Reprint, Cranbury, NJ: The Scholar's Bookshelf, 2005); John F. Luzader, *Saratoga: A Military History of the Decisive Campaign of the American Revolution* (New York: Savas Beatie, 2008); and John R. Elting, *The Battles of Saratoga* (Monmouth Beach, NJ: Philip Freneau Press, 1977).

5. Douglas R. Cubbison, *"The Artillery Never Gained More Honour": The British Artillery in the 1776 Valcour Island and 1777 Saratoga Campaigns* (Fleischmanns, NY: Purple Mountain Press, 2007), 97.

6. John Burgoyne to Guy Carleton, June 7, 1777; John Burgoyne to Lord George Germain, August 20, 1777; "Testimony of Captain Money," in Burgoyne, *State of the Expedition from Canada*, xxx–xxxi, xxi–xxiv, 41, question 19; Arthur R. Bowler, *Logistics and the Failure of the British Army in America, 1775–1783* (Princeton, NJ: Princeton University Press, 1975), 225–27. For the Americans obstructing the roads, see Helga Doblin, trans., *The Specht Journal: A Military Journal of the Burgoyne Campaign* (Westport, CT: Greenwood Press, 1995), 59.

7. Doblin, *Specht*, 57 (quote)–58, 120 n. 80–81; "A Journal of Carleton's and Burgoyne's Campaigns," *Bulletin of the Fort Ticonderoga Museum* 11 (September 1965): 316.

8. For Riedesel's original proposal, see William L. Stone, ed., *Memoirs and Letters and Journals of Major General Riedesel, During His Residence in America, translated from the Original German by Max Von Eelking*, vol. I (Albany, NY: J. Munsell, 1868), 252–54. Estimates of the size of Baum's force vary widely. Those listed here are a composite of several sources but mainly rely on Thomas M. Barker, "Braunschweigers, Hessians and Tories in the Battle of Bennington (16 August 1777): The American 'Revolution' as a Civil War," *The Hessians: Journal of the Johannes Schwalm Historical Association* 10 (2007): 39; and Paul Lawrence Stevens, "His Majesty's 'Savage' Allies: British Policy and the Northern Indians During the Revolutionary War" (PhD diss., State University of New York at Buffalo,

1984), 1194–95. For staff officers and the necessity of translators, see Michael R. Gadue, "Lieutenant Colonel Friedrich S. Baum, Officer Commanding, the Bennington Expedition: A Figure Little Known to History," *The Hessians: Journal of the Johannes Schwalm Historical Association* 11 (2008): 43–45; Helga Doblin, trans., *An Eyewitness Account of the American Revolution and New England Life: The Journal of J.F. Wasmus, German Company Surgeon, 1776–1783* (New York: Greenwood Press, 1990), 68. Wasmus provides the most complete account of the Bennington Expedition from the German perspective. For Durnford and his map, see Philip Lord Jr.'s outstanding *War Over Walloomscoick: Land Use and Settlement Pattern on the Bennington Battlefield—1777* (Albany: The University of the State of New York, 1989), especially 3, 15–16, 179–80.

9. *Collections of the Vermont Historical Society* 1 (Montpelier: Vermont Historical Society, 1870), 163–203; E.P. Walton, ed., *Records of the Council of Safety and Governor and Council of the State of Vermont to which are Prefixed the Records of the General Conventions from July 1775 to December 1777*, vol. 1 (Montpelier, VT: Steampress of J. and J.M. Poland, 1873), 130–39; Nathaniel Bouton, ed., *Provincial and State Papers: Miscellaneous Documents and Records Relating to New Hampshire at Different Periods*, vol. 8 (1874; Reprint, New York: AMS Press, Inc., 1973), 629–42.

10. For popular biographies of John Stark, see Ben Z. Rose, *John Stark: Maverick General* (Waverly, MA: TreeLine Press, 2007); and Clifton LaBree, *New Hampshire's General John Stark: Live Free or Die, Death Is Not the Worst of Evils* (Portsmouth, NH: Peter E. Randall Publisher, 2007). For the best account of his appointment and march to Bennington, see Herbert D. Foster, "Stark's Independent Command at Bennington," *Proceedings of the New York State Historical Association* 5 (1905): especially 28–30 for enlistment statistics. For additional information on New Hampshire troops and complete muster rolls, see Isaac W. Hammond, ed., *Rolls of the Soldiers in the Revolutionary War, May, 1777 to 1780: with an Appendix Embracing Names of New Hampshire Men in Massachusetts Regiments*, vol. 2 (1886; Reprint, New York: AMS Press Inc., 1973), 139–231.

11. Stone, *Memoirs and Letters*, 259–64.

12. Although some participants and historians referred to them as such, technically neither this fortification nor the one built by the dragoons atop the hill were redoubts because they were not enclosed on all four sides. Nor were they forts because they were temporary structures. The Loyalist work is actually a *crémaillère*, while the dragoon one is a cope or cowl. This book will use the term redoubt, however, because it is common usage. For

examples of the various usages and the fortifications' actual names, see Stone, *Memoirs and Letters*, 302–06; Lord, *War Over Walloomscoick*, 47–59; and Thomas M. Barker and Paul R. Huey, *The 1776–1777 Northern Campaigns of the American War for Independence and Their Sequel: Contemporary Maps of Mainly German Origins* (Fleishmanns, NY: Purple Mountain Press, 2010), 129.

13. Barker, "Braunschweigers," 19–23, 28.

14. One of the best works on the civilian response to Burgoyne's invasion is Winston Adler, ed., *Their Own Voices: Oral Accounts of Early Settlers in Washington County, New York* (Interlaken, NY: Heart of the Lakes Publishing, 1983). This book contains a selection of some of the interviews conducted by Dr. Asa Fitch, a local historian, during the 1840s.

15. Michael P. Gabriel, "'We Were in the Bennington Battle,'" *Walloomsack Review: Bennington Museum* 4 (September 2010): 39–46. For muster rolls of the Bennington militia, Samuel Herrick's Vermont Rangers and Warner's Green Mountain Boys Regiment, see John E. Goodrich, comp., *Rolls of the Soldiers in the Revolutionary War, 1775 to 1783* (Rutland, VT: The Tuttle Co., 1904), 26–27, 44–50, 107–12. There are no muster rolls for New Yorkers who fought at Bennington, and many of the Massachusetts ones, located in the State Archives in Boston, are almost illegible.

16. Michael P. Gabriel, "A Forgotten Cattle Skirmish Preceded the Battle of Bennington," *Walloomsack Review: Bennington Museum* 5 (May 2011): 35–42.

17. Various versions of Stark's quote exist but none from contemporary sources. This one is found on his equestrian statue in Manchester, New Hampshire. A marker near Stark's campsite outside Bennington quotes, "There are the red coats, and they are ours or this night Molly Stark sleeps a widow." Richard B. Smith, *The Revolutionary War in Bennington County: A History and Guide* (Charleston, SC: The History Press, 2008), 120–21.

18. For an insightful analysis of the fight at the "Tory Redoubt," see Lord, *War Over Walloomscoick*, 47–59.

19. Some sources suggest that Breymann may have purposefully delayed his march because of a dispute with Baum. Michael R. Gadue, "'Fatal Pique': The Failure of LTC Breymann to Relieve LTC Baum at Bennington, August 16, 1777, A Case of *Braunschweig* Dishonor?" *The Hessians: Journal of the Johannes Schwalm Historical Association* 12 (2009): 44–56.

20. A bat horse was an animal used to carry camp equipment.

21. John Burgoyne, *State of the Expedition*, xxxiv–xxxviii.

22. *Parliamentary Register: Or History of the Proceedings and Debates of the House of Commons: Containing an Account of the Most Interesting Speeches and Motions*, vol. 12 (London: Wilson and Co., 1802), 272–73.

23. Cornet was the lowest rank for commissioned cavalry officers.

24. "Important & fresh Intelligence from the Northern Army," *Freeman's Journal* or *New-Hampshire Gazette* [Portsmouth, NH], August 30, 1777, vol. 11, issue 12, p. 2. Courtesy of NewsBank-Readex.

25. Gail M. Potter, "Pittsfield's Fighting Parson: Thomas Allen," *New-England Galaxy* 18 (1976): 33–38.

26. "The Following Particulars of the Action between the Milita &C. and Part of the British Army of the 16th Inst. near Bennington," *Connecticut Courant* [Hartford], August 25, 1777, 3. Courtesy of NewsBank-Readex.

27. National Archives, Revolutionary War Pension and Bounty Land Warrant Application Files (2670 reels; hereafter cited as Pension Records), Magoon, Alexander W2404.

28. Pension Records, Bean, Benjamin S22115.

29. Pension Records, Wheeler, Edward S16292.

30. Pension Records, Ives, Amasa S23277.

31. Pension Records, Simson, Andrew S29459.

THE BATTLE OF BENNINGTON

32. One rod equals 16.5 feet.

33. Asa Fitch Letterbook, SARA 4136, Saratoga National Historical Park, Item 762.

34. Ibid., Item 766.

35. Pension Records, Eaton, Samuel R3212.

36. Pension Records, Austin, John S22094.

37. Pension Records, Meriam, John Jr. S18974.

38. Pension Records, Bailey, Jesse W17215.

39. Hall Park McCullough Collection, Bennington Museum, Bennington, VT.

40. Ibid.

41. Pension Records, Rudd, Joseph W17582.

42. Peter P. Woodbury, Thomas Savage and William Patten, *History of Bedford, New-Hampshire, Being Statistics, Compiled on the Occasion of the One Hundredth Anniversary of the Incorporation of the Town, May 19, 1850* (Boston, MA: Alfred Mudge, 1851), 256–57.

43. William L. Stone, ed., *Memoirs and Letters and Journals of Major General Riedesel, During His Residence in America*, translated from the original German by Max Von Eelking, vol. I (Albany, NY: J. Munsell, 1868), 299–302.

44. Pension Records, Mason, Pardon W2626.

45. Pension Records, Clark, Joseph S12487.

46. Pension Records, Mason, Nathan S9000.

47. Hall Park McCullough Collection, Bennington Museum, Bennington, VT.

48. John Hayward, *A Gazetteer of Vermont, Containing Descriptions of all the Counties, Towns, and Districts in the State, and of its Principal Mountains, Rivers, Waterfalls, Harbors, Lakes, and Curious Places, to Which are Added Statistical Accounts of Its Agriculture, Commerce, and Manufactures with a Great Variety of Other Useful Information* (Boston, MA: Tappan, Whittemore and Mason, 1849), 213–15.

49. The dock is where the horse's hind end connects with the tail.

50. Pension Records, Farnsworth, Thomas S22236.

51. Hall Park McCullough Collection, Bennington Museum, Bennington, VT.

52. Pension Records, Mason, Nathan S9000.

53. Asa Fitch Letterbook, SARA 4136, Saratoga National Historical Park, Item 766.

54. Chasseurs were light infantry soldiers specially trained and equipped for mobility.

55. "Account of an Affair which Happened near Walloon Creek, August 16, 1777," No. 43 (6.16/22b), British Records Relating to America in Microfilm, University of Pittsburgh, Pittsburgh, PA. Courtesy of Microform Academic Publishers.

OTHER ACCOUNTS

56. Pension Records, Howe, Perley S10863.

57. Levi Beardsley, *Reminiscences: Personal and Other Incidents; Early Settlement of Otsego County; Notices and Anecdotes of Public Men; Judicial, Legal and Legislative Matters; Field Sports; Dissertations and Discussions* (New York: Charles Vinten, 1852), 7–8.

58. Hall Park McCullough Collection, Bennington Museum, Bennington, VT.

59. Hayward, *Gazetteer of Vermont*, 213–15.

60. Pension Records, Moor, James W4498.

61. Pension Records, Post, William S22442.

62. Pension Records, Rowan, John S14362.

63. Pension Records, Weed, Benjamin S11715.

64. Pension Records, Stoddard, Lemuel S22538.

65. Great Britain, Audit Office, Papers of the American Loyalist Claims Commission, 1780–1835 (AO 13; hereafter cited as Audit Office); Peter Rosenbarica, Audit Office 13/24/408-409.

66. George Rosenbarica, Audit Office 13/24/406-407.
67. Samuel Anderson, Audit Office 13/11/48-48.
68. Pension Records, Dutton, Abel W24864.
69. Pension Records, Brown, Nehemiah S20648.
70. Pension Records, Partridge, Amos W2683.
71. Beardsley, *Reminiscences*, 4, 6–7, 573, 570–71.
72. Pension Records, Gage, Abel S45548.
73. Pension Records, Gage, David W14777.
74. Pension Records, Rudd, Joseph W17582.
75. Pension Records, Weed, Benjamin S11715.
76. Pension Records, Stewart, John R10154.
77. Pension Records, Wheeler, David R11380.
78. Pension Records, Meacham, Isaac W17083.
79. Pension Records, Perry, Winslow W4309.

Aftermath

80. A variation of this letter, dated August 26, 1777, is found in the Bennington Museum's Hall Park McCullough Collection.
81. Vermont Historical Society, *Proceedings of the Vermont Historical Society, October 20 and November 5, 1896* (Montpelier, VT: Argus and Patriot Press, 1896), 63.
82. John Burgoyne, *Orderly Book of Lieut. Gen. John Burgoyne, from his Entry into the State of New York until his Surrender at Saratoga, 16ᵗʰ Oct., 1777*, edited by E.B. O'Callaghan (Albany, NY: J. Munsell, 1860), 82–84.
83. John Burgoyne, *State of the Expedition*, xxiv–xxv.

Appendix A

84. Charles Carleton Coffin, *The History of Boscawen and Webster from 1733 to 1878* (Concord, NH: Republican Press, Asso., 1878), 262; Pension Records, Abell, Thomas R8.
85. Asa Fitch Letterbook, SARA 4136, Saratoga National Historical Park, Item 763; Thomas Jefferson to Thomas Mann Randolph Jr., June 5, 1791, in Julian P. Boyd, ed., *The Papers of Thomas Jefferson*, 20 (Princeton, NJ: Princeton University Press, 1982), 464–66; "Bennington Battle Ground," *Republican Star and General Advertiser* [Easton, MD], November 23, 1830, vol. 32, issue 13, p. 1, Early American Newspapers online (accessed June 5, 2006).

86. Pension Records, Dewey, Samuel S9327; Sutton, Stephen BLW 49467-160-55.

87. Quoted in Sarah J. Purcell, *Sealed with Blood: War, Sacrifice, and Memory in Revolutionary America* (Philadelphia: University of Pennsylvania Press, 2002), 130; also see 20, 82–85, 128–29, 155–56, 188–89.

88. Pension Records, Brown, Daniel W21710.

89. Josiah Wright, David Fay, Jonas Galusha, Jonathan Robinson and William Towner to John Stark, August 16, 1806, in Caleb Stark, *Memoir and Official Correspondence of Gen. John Stark, with Notices of Several Other Officers of the Revolution. Also a Biography of Capt. Phineas Stevens, and of Col. Robert Rogers, with an Account of His Services in America During the "Seven Years' War"* (1877; Reprint, Bowie, MD: Heritage Books, 1999), 310–11; Gideon Olin, Jonathan Robinson and David Fay to John Stark, July 22, 1809, 311–12.

90. Pension Records, Rudd, Joseph W17582.

91. John Stark, "At My Quarters, at Derry Field, July 31ˢᵗ, 1809" *American Monitor* [Plattsburgh, NY], September 29, 1809, vol. 1, issue 9, p. 3, Early American Newspapers online (accessed May 19, 2006). Courtesy of NewsBank-Readex.

Selected Bibliography

Manuscripts

American Papers in the House of Lords Records, British Records Relating to America in Microfilm. University of Pittsburgh, Pittsburgh, PA.

Asa Fitch Letterbook, SARA 4136. Saratoga National Historical Park, Stillwater, NY.

Great Britain. Audit Office. Papers of the American Loyalist Claims Commission, 1780–1835 (AO 13). David Library of the American Revolution, Washington Crossing, PA.

Hall Park McCullough Collection, Bennington Museum, Bennington, VT.

Thomas Jefferson Papers. Library of Congress, American Memory. http://memory.loc.gov/ammem/collections/jefferson_papers/index.html (accessed April 13, 2011).

Warrant Application Files. United States. National Archives. Revolutionary War Pension and Bounty-Land. David Library of the American Revolution, Washington Crossing, PA.

Printed Primary Sources

Adler, Winston, ed. *Their Own Voices: Oral Accounts of Early Settlers in Washington County, New York.* Interlaken, NY: Heart of the Lakes Publishing, 1983.

Aichinger, Peter, trans., ed. *At War with the Americans: The Journal of Claude-Nicolas-Guillaume de Lorimier.* Victoria, BC: Press Porcepic, 1981.

Barker, Thomas M., and Paul R. Huey, eds. *The 1776–1777 Northern Campaigns of the American War for Independence and Their Sequel: Contemporary Maps of Mainly German Origin*. Fleischmanns, NY: Purple Mountain Press, 2010.

Bouton, Nathaniel, ed. *Provincial and State Papers: Miscellaneous Documents and Records Relating to New Hampshire at Different Periods*. Vol. 8. 1874. Reprint, New York: AMS Press, Inc., 1973.

Boyd, Julian P., ed. *The Papers of Thomas Jefferson*. Vol. 20. Princeton, NJ: Princeton University Press, 1982.

Burgoyne, John. *A State of the Expedition from Canada, as Laid before the House of Commons, by Lieutenant-General Burgoyne, and Verified by Evidence; with a Collection of Authentic Documents, and an Addition of Many Circumstances Which were Prevented from Appearing before the House by the Prorogation of Parliament*. London: J. Almon, 1780.

Collections of the Vermont Historical Society. Vol. 1. Montpelier: Vermont Historical Society, 1870.

Dann, John C. ed. *The Revolution Remembered: Eyewitness Accounts of the War for Independence*. Chicago: University of Chicago Press, 1980.

Doblin, Helga, trans. *An Eyewitness Account of the American Revolution and New England Life: The Journal of J.F. Wasmus, German Company Surgeon, 1776–1783*. New York: Greenwood Press, 1990.

————. *The Specht Journal: A Military Journal of the Burgoyne Campaign*. Westport, CT: Greenwood Press, 1995.

Goodrich, John E., comp. *Rolls of the Soldiers in the Revolutionary War, 1775 to 1783*. Rutland, VT: The Tuttle Co., 1904.

Hammond, Isaac W., ed. *Rolls of the Soldiers in the Revolutionary War, May, 1777 to 1780: with an Appendix Embracing Names of New Hampshire Men in Massachusetts Regiments*. Vol. 2. 1886. Reprint, New York: AMS Press Inc., 1973.

"A Journal of Carleton's and Burgoyne's Campaigns." *Bulletin of the Fort Ticonderoga Museum* 11 (December 1964–September 1965): 234–69; 306–35; 12 (March 1966): 5–62.

Parliamentary Register: Or History of the Proceedings and Debates of the House of Commons: Containing an Account of the Most Interesting Speeches and Motions. Vol. 12. London: Wilson and Co., 1802.

Rogers, Horatio, ed. *Hadden's Journal and Orderly Book: A Journal Kept in Canada and Upon Burgoyne's Campaign in 1776 and 1777, by James M. Hadden; also Orders Kept by Him and Issued by Sir Guy Carleton, John Burgoyne, and William Phillips, in 1776, 1777 and 1778, with an Explanatory Chapter and Notes*. 1884. Reprint, Freeport, NY: Books for Libraries Press, 1970.

Stark, Caleb. *Memoir and Official Correspondence of Gen. John Stark, With Notices of Several Other Officers of the Revolution. Also a Biography of Capt. Phineas Stevens, and of Col. Robert Rogers, with an Account of His Services in America During the "Seven Years' War."* 1877. Reprint, Bowie, MD: Heritage Books, 1999.

Stone, William L., ed. *Memoirs and Letters and Journals of Major General Riedesel, During his Residence in America, translated from the Original German by Max Von Eelking.* Vol. 1. Albany, NY: J. Munsell, 1868.

Walton, E.P., ed. *Records of the Council of Safety and Governor and Council of the State of Vermont to which are Prefixed the Records of the General Conventions from July 1775 to December 1777.* Vol. 1. Montpelier, VT: Steampress of J. [and J.M.] Poland, 1873.

NEWSPAPERS

American Monitor. Early American Newspapers online (accessed May 19, 2006).

Connecticut Courant

Freeman's Journal or New-Hampshire Gazette

Republican Star and General Advertiser. Early American Newspapers online (accessed June 5, 2006).

SECONDARY SOURCES

Barker, Thomas M. "Braunschweigers, Hessians and Tories in the Battle of Bennington (16 August 1777): The American 'Revolution' as a Civil War." *The Hessians: Journal of the Johannes Schwalm Historical Association* 10 (2007): 13–39.

Beardsley, Levi. *Reminiscences: Personal and Other Incidents; Early Settlement of Otsego County; Notices and Anecdotes of Public Men; Judicial, Legal and Legislative Matters; Field Sports; Dissertations and Discussions.* New York: Charles Vinten, 1852.

Bowler, R. Arthur. *Logistics and the Failure of the British Army in America, 1775–1783.* Princeton, NJ: Princeton University Press, 1975.

Burns, Brian. "Massacre or Muster? Burgoyne's Indians and the Militia at Bennington." *Vermont History* 45 (1977): 133–44.

Coffin, Charles Carleton. *The History of Boscawen and Webster from 1733 to 1878.* Concord, NH: Republican Press, Associated, 1878.

Cubbison, Douglas R. *The American Northern Theater Army in 1776: The Ruin and Reconstruction of the Continental Force.* Jefferson, NC: McFarland & Company, Inc., Publishers, 2010.

————. *"The Artillery Never Gained More Honour": The British Artillery in the 1776 Valcour Island and 1777 Saratoga Campaigns.* Fleischmanns, NY: Purple Mountain Press, 2007.

Elting, John R. *The Battles of Saratoga.* Monmouth Beach, NJ: Philip Freneau Press, 1977.

Foster, Herbert D. "Stark's Independent Command at Bennington." *Proceedings of the New York State Historical Association* 5 (1905): 24–95.

Gabriel, Michael P. "A Forgotten Cattle Skirmish Preceded the Battle of Bennington." *Walloomsack Review: Bennington Museum* 5 (May 2011): 35–42.

————. *Major General Richard Montgomery: The Making of an American Hero.* Madison, NJ: Fairleigh Dickinson University Press, 2002.

————. "'We Were in the Bennington Battle.'" *Walloomsack Review: Bennington Museum* 4 (September 2010): 39–46.

Gadue, Michael R. "'Fatal Pique': The Failure of LTC Breymann to Relieve LTC Baum at Bennington, August 16, 1777, A Case of *Braunschweig* Dishonor?" *The Hessians: Journal of the Johannes Schwalm Historical Association* 12 (2009): 44–56.

————. "Lieutenant Colonel Friedrich S. Baum, Officer Commanding, the Bennington Expedition: A Figure Little Known to History." *The Hessians: Journal of the Johannes Schwalm Historical Association* 11 (2008): 37–54.

Ketchum, Richard M. *Saratoga: Turning Point of America's Revolutionary War.* New York: Henry Holt and Co., 1997.

LaBree, Clifton. *New Hampshire's General John Stark: Live Free or Die, Death Is Not the Worst of Evils.* Portsmouth, NH: Peter E. Randall Publisher, 2007.

Lord, Philip, Jr. *War Over Walloomscoick: Land Use and Settlement Pattern on the Bennington Battlefield—1777.* Albany, NY: The State Education Department, 1989.

Luzader, John F. *Saratoga: A Military History of the Decisive Campaign of the American Revolution.* New York: Savas Beatie, 2008.

Nickerson, Hoffman. *The Turning Point of the Revolution, Or Burgoyne in America.* 1928. Reprint, Cranbury, NJ: The Scholar's Bookshelf, 2005.

Petersen, James E. *Seth Warner: "This Extraordinary American..."* Middlebury, VT: Dunmore House, 2001.

Potter, Gail M. "Pittsfield's Fighting Parson: Thomas Allen." *New-England Galaxy* 18 (1976): 33–38.

Purcell, Sarah J. *Sealed with Blood: War, Sacrifice, and Memory in Revolutionary America*. Philadelphia: University of Pennsylvania Press, 2002.

Resch, John. *Suffering Soldiers: Revolutionary War Veterans, Moral Sentiment, and Political Culture in the Early Republic*. Amherst: University of Massachusetts Press, 1999.

Rose, Ben Z. *John Stark: Maverick General*. Waverly, MA: TreeLine Press, 2007.

Smith, Richard B. *The Revolutionary War in Bennington County: A History and Guide*. Charleston, SC: The History Press, 2008.

Spargo, John. *The Bennington Battle Monument: Its Story and Its Meaning*. Rutland, VT: The Tuttle Co., 1925.

Stevens, Paul Lawrence. "His Majesty's 'Savage' Allies: British Policy and the Northern Indians During the Revolutionary War." PhD diss., State University of New York at Buffalo, 1984.

Strach, Stephen G. *Some Sources for the Study of Loyalists and Canadian Participation in the Military Campaign of Lieutenant-General John Burgoyne 1777*. N.p.: Eastern National Park and Monument Association, 1983.

Taylor, Maureen. *The Last Muster: Images of the Revolutionary War Generation*. Kent, OH: Kent State University Press, 2010.

Vermont Historical Society. *Proceedings of the Vermont Historical Society, October 20 and November 5, 1896*. Montpelier, VT: Argus and Patriot Press, 1896.

Ward, Christopher. *The War of the Revolution*. 2 vols. New York: The Macmillan Co., 1952.

Williams, John. *The Battle of Hubbardton: The American Rebels Stem the Tide*. 1988. Reprint, Montpelier: Vermont Division for Historic Preservation, 2002.

Woodbury, Peter P., Thomas Savage and William Patten. *History of Bedford, New-Hampshire, Being Statistics, Compiled on the Occasion of the One Hundredth Anniversary of the Incorporation of the Town, May 19, 1850*. Boston, MA: Alfred Mudge, 1851.

About the Author

Michael P. Gabriel, a professor of history at Kutztown University, grew up in Bradford, Pennsylvania. He earned his BS at Clarion University, his MA at St. Bonaventure and his PhD at Penn State. He is a member of the Pennsylvania Historical Association, the Society of Military History, the Johannes Schwalm Historical Association and the Kutztown Area Historical Society. His other works include authoring *Major General Richard Montgomery: The Making of an American Hero* (2002) and co-editing *Quebec During the American Invasion, 1775–1776: The Journal of François Baby, Gabriel Taschereau, and Jenkin Williams* (2005). Gabriel has also published numerous reviews and essays and has contributed entries to a variety of reference works. He and his wife, Sandy, live near Kutztown with their daughter, Katie.